First Workshop on Ever Evolving NLP (EvoNLP 2022)

Abu Dhabi, United Arab Emirates and Online
7 December 2022

ISBN: 978-1-7138-9108-6

Printed from e-media with permission by:

Curran Associates, Inc.
57 Morehouse Lane
Red Hook, NY 12571

Some format issues inherent in the e-media version may also appear in this print version.

Printed with permission by Curran Associates, Inc. (2024)

For permission requests, please contact the Association for Computational Linguistics at the address below.

Association for Computational Linguistics
209 N. Eighth Street
Stroudsburg, Pennsylvania 18360

Phone: 1-570-476-8006
Fax: 1-570-476-0860

acl@aclweb.org

Additional copies of this publication are available from:

Curran Associates, Inc.
57 Morehouse Lane
Red Hook, NY 12571 USA
Phone: 845-758-0400
Fax: 845-758-2633
Email: curran@proceedings.com
Web: www.proceedings.com

EvoNLP 2022

The First Workshop on Ever Evolving NLP

Proceedings of the Workshop

December 7, 2022

The EvoNLP organizers gratefully acknowledge the support from the following sponsors.

Sponsored by

Snap Inc.

Preface by the Workshop Organizers

We are excited to welcome you to EvoNLP 2022, the 1st Workshop on Ever Evolving NLP. This workshop follows a hybrid format, and is being held on December 7, 2022, co-located with EMNLP 2022, which will also follow a hybrid format (Abu Dhabi and remote).

EvoNLP is a forum to discuss the challenges posed by the dynamic nature of language in the specific context of the current NLP paradigm, dominated by language models. This year, the program includes a regular session, a session dedicated to the time-aware Word-in-Context classification shared task, as well as non-archival presentations and Findings of EMNLP papers. Finally, are delighted to have the following renowned invited speakers: Eunsol Choi, Jacob Eisenstein, Adam Jatowt, Ozan Sener and Nazneen Rajani.

15 papers will be presented at EvoNLP. In particular, 3 research papers, 5 TempoWiC system description papers, 4 Findings of EMNLP papers, and 3 non-archival submissions. These papers cover a variety of topics, for example few shot learning using incremental approaches, clustering techniques for dynamic topic discovery, construction of temporal benchmarks, or leveraging time-dependent features for offensive language detection. Regarding the TempoWiC shared task, our participants leveraged techniques such as multitask learning, mixture-of-experts or generative approaches.

We would like to thank the Program Committee members for their support of this event in form of reviewing and feedback, without whom we would not be able to ensure the overall quality of the workshop.

Organizing Committee

Organizers

Francesco Barbieri, Snap Inc.
Jose Camacho-Collados, Cardiff University
Bhuwan Dhingra, Duke University
Luis Espinosa-Anke, Cardiff University / AMPLYFI
Elena Gribovskaya, DeepMind
Angeliki Lazaridou, DeepMind
Daniel Loureiro, Cardiff University
Leonardo Neves, Snap Inc.

Program Committee

Workshop Reviewers

Alessandro Raganato, University of Milano-Bicocca
Dimosthenis Antypas, Cardiff University
David Vilares, University of A Coruña
Ian Stewart, University of Michigan
Indira Sen, GESIS, Leibnitz Institute
David Jurgens, University of Michigan
Sebastian Ruder, Google
Sanjaya Wijeratne, TrueNorth
Steven Schockaert, Cardiff University

Shared Task Reviewers

Daniel Loureiro, Cardiff University
Jose Camacho-Collados, Cardiff University
Chenyang Lyu, Dublin City University
Elizaveta Tukhtina, HSE University
Ze Chen, NetEase, Inc.

Keynote Talk: Knowledge-rich NLP models in a dynamic real world

Eunsol Choi
UT-Austin

Abstract: To address knowledge-rich tasks such as question answering, NLP models should combine knowledge from multiple sources – memorized knowledge in the language model (LM), and passages retrieved from an evidence corpus. Prior work assumed information stored in various sources is consistent with each other. Yet, a mismatch in knowledge sources is common in the real world: some sources are updated while others remain stale, and different sources can interpret the same question differently or propose differing opinions. How should we resolve such complex knowledge conflicts? In this talk, I will describe our recent work on (1) an evaluation framework for updating knowledge in LMs and (2) how state-of-the-art models behave under knowledge conflicts. I will conclude my talk with paths for handling real-world scenarios, continual learning of models and calibrating them to avoid answering when provided with incomplete or conflicting information.

Bio: Eunsol Choi is an assistant professor in the Computer Science department at the University of Texas at Austin and a visiting researcher at Google AI. Her research area spans natural language processing and machine learning. She is particularly interested in interpreting and reasoning about text in a rich real-world context. She received a Ph.D. from University of Washington and B.A from Cornell University. She is a recipient of Facebook research fellowship, Google faculty research award, and outstanding paper award at EMNLP 2021.

Keynote Talk: What can we learn from language change?

Jacob Eisenstein
Google

Abstract: Language changes are shaped by world events and social structures. With an increasingly rich set of resources for studying text over time, this raises the possibility of reverse-engineering language change to uncover new insights about the world. This talk will survey work on diachronic corpora of social media, historical newspapers, and scientific research papers. We use these corpora to build models of cultural transmission between US cities, the effects of social media platforms' policies and norms, the leaders of the movement to abolish slavery in the United States, and which ACL papers are likely to get the most citations in the future. Collaborators include Sandeep Soni, Umashanthi Pavalanathan, Lauren F. Klein, Kristina Lerman, and David Bamman.

Bio: Jacob Eisenstein is a research scientist at Google, where he is focused on making language technology more robust and trustworthy. He was previously on the faculty of the Georgia Institute of Technology, where he supervised six successful doctoral dissertations, received the NSF CAREER Award for research on computational sociolinguistics, and wrote a textbook on natural language processing. He completed his Ph.D. at MIT, winning the George M. Sprowls award for a dissertation on computational models of speech and gesture. Thanks to his brief appearance in the documentary film If These Knishes Could Talk, Jacob has a Bacon number of 2.
https://jacobeisenstein.github.io/

Keynote Talk: Automatic Question Answering over Temporal News Collections

Adam Jatowt
University of Innsbruck

Abstract: The field of automatic question answering has been rapidly advancing recently. The existing QA approaches are however generally working on synchronic document collections such as Wikipedia, Web data or short-term news corpora. This talk is about our latest efforts in automatic question answering over diachronic news collections composed of articles published over several decades. We will first discuss an unsupervised re-ranking approach that works by utilizing temporal information embedded in the temporal document collection. Next, we will introduce a solution for finding the occurrence dates of events described in input questions based on the underlying news dataset. Finally, we will introduce ArchivalQA - a large-scale question answering dataset which has been automatically created from a two decades' long news article collection, and which contains over 500k question-answer pairs. The dataset has been processed to remove temporally ambiguous questions for which more than one correct answer exist.

Bio: Adam Jatowt is a Professor at the Department of Computer Science and Digital Science Center at the University of Innsbruck. He received his Ph.D. in Information Science and Technology from the University of Tokyo, Japan in 2005. Before moving to Austria, Adam worked at Kyoto University as an Assistant and later as an Associate Professor. His research interests include information retrieval, natural language processing, digital libraries, and digital humanities. Adam has published over 180 research papers in international conferences and journals. He is an editorial board member of IP&M, JASIST, IJDL, JIIS, and IEEE JoSC journals. Adam has received the Vannevar Bush Best Paper Award at JCDL2021, the best short paper award at ECIR2018, and the best demo award at ECIR2019.

Keynote Talk: Going from Continual Learning Algorithms to Continual Learning Systems

Ozan Sener
Apple

Abstract: We envision continual learning systems to interact with humans, with each other, and the physical world through time – and continue to learn and adapt as they do. On the other hand, we develop and benchmark continual learning algorithms, hoping they will be the future founding blocks of such systems. I will argue that going from algorithmic to system thinking requires carefully questioning various assumptions. Consider the common assumption of storage being fixed and limited through the agent's lifetime. The economics of data storage suggests that the cost of storing data decreases over time and is negligible compared to the cost of computing. Following this economics, computing systems around us are not constrained by storage but rather by computation. This motivates us to explore online continual learning with computation constraints instead of storage constraints. Using this new setting, we set a new state of the art on the largest large-scale continual learning datasets.

Bio: Ozan Sener is interested in machine learning and its applications in computer vision and robotics. Specifically, Ozan is interested in designing machine learning algorithms which can process large-amount of multimodal information with no/weak supervision.
Ozan is a research scientist at Apple. Ozan received his PhD from Cornell University, advised by Ashutosh Saxena. Following the advisor's move, Ozan spent three beautiful years at Stanford AI Lab as a visiting PhD student (2015-2016) and a postdoc (2017) working with Silvio Savarese. Ozan obtained his BSc and MSc degrees from METU.

Keynote Talk: Takeaways from a systematic study of 75K models on Hugging Face

Nazneen Fatema Rajani
Hugging Face

Abstract: Language models trained using transformers dominate the NLP model landscape, making Hugging Face (HF) the de facto hub for sharing, benchmarking, and evaluating NLP models. The HF hub provides a rich resource for understanding how language models evolved, opening up research questions on how factors such as model age and documentation affect their usage. We conducted a systematic study of the hub to glean insights into the ever-evolving model landscape and what factors affect model usage. We also studied model documentation for semantic drifts, and observed an evolution in the use of specific keywords (such as "train," "evaluate," "impact"), indicating a paradigm shift from model-centric to more data-centric ML development. In this talk, I will give a macro-level view of this evolving model landscape and discuss the results from our systematic study of 75K HF models.

Bio: Nazneen is a Research Lead at HuggingFace, a startup with a mission to democratize ML, leading data-centric ML research which involves systematically analyzing, curating, and automatically annotating data. Before HF, she worked at Salesforce Research with Richard Socher and led a team of researchers focused on building robust natural language generation systems based on LLMs. She completed her Ph.D. in CS at UT-Austin with Prof. Ray Mooney.
Nazneen has over 30 papers published at ACL, EMNLP, NAACL, NeurIPs, and ICLR and has her research covered by Quanta magazine, VentureBeat, SiliconAngle, ZDNet, and Datanami. She is also teaching a course on interpreting ML models with Corise – http://corise.com/go/nazneen. More details about her work can be found here https://www.nazneenrajani.com/.

Table of Contents

Program

Wednesday, December 7, 2022

09:00 - 09:30	*Opening remarks*
09:30 - 10:00	*Jacob Eisenstein - What can we learn from language change?*
10:00 - 10:30	*Eunsol Choi - Knowledge-rich NLP models in a dynamic real world*
10:30 - 11:00	*Adam Jatowt - Automatic Question Answering over Temporal News Collections*
11:00 - 12:30	*Workshop poster session (virtual and on-site)*
12:30 - 14:00	*Lunch break*
14:00 - 15:00	*Findings and non-archival session*
15:00 - 15:30	*Coffee break*
15:30 - 16:00	*Nazneen Rajani - Takeaways from a systematic study of 75K models on Hugging Face*
16:00 - 16:30	*Ozan Sener - Going from Continual Learning Algorithms to Continual Learning Systems*
16:30 - 17:00	*Workshop oral session*
17:00 - 17:30	*Shared task session*
17:30 - 18:00	*Best paper awards and closing*

MLLabs-LIG at TempoWiC 2022: A Generative Approach for Examining Temporal Meaning Shift

Chenyang Lyu[†*] **Yongxin Zhou**[‡*] **Tianbo Ji**[†]
[†] School of Computing, Dublin City University, Dublin, Ireland
[‡] LIG, Univ. Grenoble Alpes, Grenoble, France
{chenyang.lyu2, tianbo.ji2}@mail.dcu.ie, yongxin.zhou@univ-grenoble-alpes.fr

Abstract

In this paper, we present our system for the EvoNLP 2022 shared task Temporal Meaning Shift (TempoWiC). Different from the typically used discriminative model, we propose a generative approach based on pre-trained generation models. The basic architecture of our system is a seq2seq model where the input sequence consists of two documents followed by a question asking whether the meaning of target word changed or not, the target output sequence is a declarative sentence describing the meaning of target word changed or not. The experimental results on TempoWiC test set show that our best system (with time information) obtained an accuracy and Macro-F1 score of 68.09% and 62.59% respectively, which ranked 12th among all submitted systems. The results have shown the plausibility of using generation model for WiC tasks, meanwhile also indicate there's still room for further improvement.

1 Introduction

The EvoNLP Shared Task Temporal Meaning Shift (TempoWiC) (Loureiro et al., 2022) aims to judge whether the meaning of a target word in a pair of sentences (two tweets in this case) change or not. Different from original WiC (Word-in-Context) task, TempoWiC takes into account the temporal information in the text, as tweets in each pair are with the date when they are posted. Therefore, that brings new challenges into this task - *how to make use of the temporal information in the tweets?*

Unlike Conventional approaches for WiC tasks that typically adopt discriminative models (such as BERT or RoBERTa) with an input consisting of a pair of sentences (Devlin et al., 2019; Liu et al., 2019; Loureiro et al., 2021), here we propose a generative approach. In our approach we treat the temporal information in tweets as normal words without complicated designation for task schema, aiming at exploiting the natural language understanding (NLU) capability of the pre-trained generation model (Radford et al., 2019; Lewis et al., 2020). Moreover, that could potentially inspire further developments for such tasks based on large language models (LLMs) such as GPT-3 (Brown et al., 2020) with Prompt Learning which has been the focus of the community recently due to its superior zero-shot performance (Liu et al., 2021).

Specifically, for the input sequence we concatenate two tweets which are followed by a question asking whether the meaning of the target word change or not. The output sequence is a declarative sentence stating whether the meaning of the target word changed or not in the two tweets. In our approach, TempoWiC is framed as a generative QA task and the construction of the data follows the manner of template-based Question Generation (Lewis and Fan, 2019; Heilman and Smith, 2009; Fabbri et al., 2020; Lyu et al., 2021). With the training data constructed in such format, we fine-tune the pre-trained generation models as a seq2seq model using a vanilla autoregressive generation objective (Sutskever et al., 2014; Johnson et al., 2017; Yang et al., 2019).

We submitted two systems (one with time information and the other one without time information) to TempoWiC for evaluation. Results show that our best best system (with time information) on the TempoWiC test set obtained an accuracy and Macro-F1 score of 68.09% and 62.59% respectively, which slightly outperforms the other system without time information with an accuracy and Macro-F1 score of 68.02% and 61.14%. Based on the evaluation results on TempoWiC test set, we found that pre-trained generation models are capable of capturing the meaning shift of target word in context. Besides, results also show that time information (date of each tweet) can provide further improvement for performance, showing the

*These authors contributed equally to this work.

Proceedings of the The First Workshop on Ever Evolving NLP (EvoNLP), pages 1 - 6
December 7, 2022 ©2022 Association for Computational Linguistics

importance of temporal information. In the rest of this paper, we will introduce the architecture of our system and give more detailed experimental results.

2 Methodology

In this section, we briefly introduce how TempoWiC task is formulated in this paper and how to train our system.

2.1 Task formulation

We frame the TempoWiC task as a seq2seq generation task where the source sequence consists of two tweets followed by a question, the target sequence is a declarative sentence. Moreover, in order to avoid the generation of naive output (e.g., all same output), we have some specific designation for the input and output sequence: the question in the source sequence must be an interrogative sentence specific to the target word, also the target sequence has to include the target word. As a generative approach, the format of input and output sequence of our system are as follows:

- **Input**: *Tweet1 - Tweet2 - Question: Does the meaning of word X change?*
- **Output**: *Is the meaning of X different in the last two tweets?*

Note *X* is the target word that we wish to examine whether its meaning changed or not in the two tweets. For instance, a concrete example in such format is shown as follows:

Input: *Tweet-1: The book in 19th century is fantastic...... Date: 2018-03. Tweet-2: Need help to book the next-day flight...... Date: 2019-03. Question: Is the meaning of* ***book*** *different in the last two tweets?*

Output: *Answer: No, the meaning of* ***book*** *is not the same.*

where we highlight the target word ***book***, of which the presence in the input and output sequence is essential for PLMs to learn how to measure the meaning shift of the target word.

2.2 Training objective

Our training objective is to minimize the Negative Log Likelihood Loss with respect to the parameters θ of our autoregressive generation systems:

$$J(\theta) = -logP(q|c,a) = \sum_i logP(a_i|a_{<i},c,q) \quad (1)$$

where a is our target sequence *answer*, c is the *context* (two tweets) and q is the *question*.

3 Experiment

Model	Accuracy	Macro F-1
BART-base	65.91	63.33
BART-large	69.19	65.72

Table 1: Performance of BART-base and BART-large on TempoWiC validation set.

3.1 Data

The training, validation and test set of TempoWiC data contain 1428, 396 and 10000 examples respectively. We show the average length of the two tweets in TempoWiC dataset in Table 2, where we found that the average length of the first tweet is typically longer than the second tweet in all splits especially in validation set.

3.2 Training Setup

We employ BART (Lewis et al., 2020) as our seq2seq model, which is Pre-trained Language Models (PLMs) that have been shown to be effective in various natural language generation tasks (Lai et al., 2021; Lewis et al., 2021; Zhou et al., 2022). Our implementation is based on BART-base and BART-large (Lewis et al., 2020) from Huggingface (Wolf et al., 2020). We train our system with a learning rate of 3×10^{-5} for 10 epochs, the batch size is set to 4. We use a maximum source sequence length of 512 and a maximum target sequence length of 64.

3.3 Results

We report the results on validation set of BART-base and BART-large in Table 1, the results show that BART-large outperforms BART-base by 3.28 accuracy and 4.39 Macro F-1 score. Therefore, our two submitted systems are based on BART-large. Table 3 shows the results of the official TempoWiC Competition Leaderboard (29 September 2022), our best system (with time information) ranked 12th with an accuracy and Macro F-1 score of 68.09% and 62.59% respectively, meanwhile our

Split	Number of Examples	Avg. Len. of Tweet-1	Avg. Len. of Tweet-2	Number of Target Words
Train	1428	31.79	30.68	15
Validation	396	28.20	24.29	4
Test	10000	26.74	25.70	15

Table 2: Average length for the tweets in the train, validation and test set as well as the number of target words of TempoWiC dataset.

Rank	User/Baseline	Accuracy	Macro-F1
1	dma	78.34%	77.05%
2	macd	77.53%	76.60%
3	zackchen	75.49%	74.87%
4	dmi	74.13%	73.37%
5	wangkangxu	73.46%	73.08%
6	vol	73.66%	72.54%
-	TimeLMs - SIM	74.07%	70.33%
7	lisatukhtina	70.94%	70.09%
8	subhamkumar	70.47%	69.79%
9	mahhars	70.47%	69.79%
10	eternalfeather	69.18%	68.49%
-	RoBERTa-L - SIM	72.98%	67.09%
11	nst	72.51%	63.75%
12	**MLLabs-LIG**	**68.09%**	**62.59%**
13	yashamz	63.00%	61.97%
14	pgatti	66.67%	59.38%
-	RoBERTa-L - FT	66.49%	59.10%
15	adityakane	67.41%	57.94%
-	TimeLMs - FT	66.46%	57.70%
16	PaulTrust	62.66%	55.38%
17	virk	55.13%	54.25%
18	daminglu123	50.78%	50.13%
-	Random	50.00%	50.00%
-	All True	36.59%	26.79%

Table 3: Official TempoWiC Codalab Competition Leaderboard (29 September 2022). Baselines on the TempoWiC are marked in lightgray with their results: **TimeLMs - SIM** is Logistic Regression based on Similarity of Contextual Embeddings from TimeLMs-2019-90M (pooled following LMMS-SP); **RoBERTa-L - SIM** is Logistic Regression based on Similarity of Contextual Embeddings from RoBERTa-Large (pooled following LMMS-SP); **RoBERTa-L - FT** is Fine-tuned RoBERTa-Large (following configuration used in SuperGLUE) and **TimeLMs - FT** is TimeLMs - FT Fine-tuned TimeLMs-2019-90M (following configuration used in SuperGLUE). Besides, **Random** means predictions are randomly assigned T/F and **All True** refers that All instances assigned T (Loureiro et al., 2022).

system without time information obtained an accuracy and Macro F-1 score of 68.02% and 61.14%. Our generative approach outperforms the baselines including *RoBERTa-L-FT*, *TimeLMs-FT*, *Random* and *All True*, whereas underperforms compared to the baselines *TimeLMs-SIM* and *RoBERTa-L-SIM*.

From the results shown in Table 1 and Table 3, we have three main findings:

- The use of a generative approach for the WiC task is plausible as the results show that our system outperforms several competitive baseline models based on BERT
- Temporal information has positive effect in predicting whether the meaning of the target word changed or not
- Larger PLMs is more likely to produce higher performance, indicating further improvement can be achieved with increasing the size of PLMs

Tweet-1	Tweet-2	Target Word	Label	Prediction
I can't believe impostor syndrome just tried to equate the tattoo I'm about to get that symbolizes something I studied for 3.5 years + graduated with a 1.7 in to trying a sport once and getting a tattoo about it, just because I'm sort of mediocre at the actual subject (2019-09)	*'damn I was in a game of among us and I was SURE red did it like I saw red kill pink but hen red wasn't the impostor??? wtf my mother did suspect I am mildly colorblind' (2020-09)*	*impostor*	0	0
Today run bts was epic as the Christmas one or the one in lotte world, the boys competitiveness is (2019-09)	*so we've got namjoon's live on youtube, cns 1 year anniversary, the lotte online concert, tiktok ot7, and the new album announcement today (2020-09)*	*lotte*	1	0
i watched that lotte world run episode again and now i want to go back and ride french revolution it was so much fun :((2019-09)	*Dude I still haven't recovered from lotte family I'm half asleep how do I even react to be? (2020-09)*	*lotte*	1	0
COLTS/TEXANS TRIVIA for 4 primo seats to the showdown this Thursday night + $5k to help toward travel: Name the Colts player who recovered his own onside kick vs. Houston AND the final score!! (Note, the $ will be received at the game). Alyssa's hat pick! (2019-11)	*'Somali guys used to be very good tukicheza futa either primo ama zile matches za estate. I wonder why à good number of them never end up in professional football clubs or the national team.' (2020-1)*	*primo*	0	0
In 2016 Sheila Dixon wanted a recount, Pugh had no integrity. She talked greasy about Sheila. Karma is a real bitch huh Pugh? (2019-11)	*Delaying the transition only affects the suffering of Americans during Covid. All thank to Trump's false claims. Can't wait to see #Georgia recount show Trump losing. #TrumpConcede' (2020-11)*	*recount*	1	1

Table 4: Examples from TempoWiC validation set with corresponding predictions from our system, where 1 represents the meaning of the target word has not changed whereas 0 represents meaning of the target word has changed.

3.4 Error analysis

We show some examples with corresponding predictions in Table 4. From Table 4, we found that our proposed generative approach is capable of detecting most meaning shift for the target word (for example *impostor*, *recount* and *primo*). However, it still has difficulties in some cases, such as *lotte*, as shown in the two examples in Table 4 where our system predicts that the meaning of *lotte* has not changed - which is not true. Experimental results as well as error analysis show that pre-trained generative models still have difficulties recognizing some language variation, which needs to be addressed in future developments. We think the fast evolving and changing meanings of words on the web, especially on social media, make this task even more challenging.

4 Conclusion

In this paper, we present a generative approach based on Pre-trained Language Models for the TempoWiC task. Experimental results show the plausibility of using pre-trained generative model for the TempoWiC task, which could potentially inspire further developments based on more pre-trained models.

Limitations

While pre-trained generative models exhibit strong capabilities for natural language understanding with prompts (Liu et al., 2021), there are still issues to be addressed such as explainability, controllability of outputs as these systems fully reply on the generative ability of pre-trained models. Moreover, how to correctly understand instructions in context/prompt (such as questions) is still challenging for pre-trained models (Min et al., 2022; Jang et al., 2022).

References

Tom Brown, Benjamin Mann, Nick Ryder, Melanie Subbiah, Jared D Kaplan, Prafulla Dhariwal, Arvind Neelakantan, Pranav Shyam, Girish Sastry, Amanda Askell, Sandhini Agarwal, Ariel Herbert-Voss, Gretchen Krueger, Tom Henighan, Rewon Child, Aditya Ramesh, Daniel Ziegler, Jeffrey Wu, Clemens Winter, Chris Hesse, Mark Chen, Eric Sigler, Mateusz Litwin, Scott Gray, Benjamin Chess, Jack Clark, Christopher Berner, Sam McCandlish, Alec Radford, Ilya Sutskever, and Dario Amodei. 2020. Language models are few-shot learners. In *Advances in Neural Information Processing Systems*, volume 33, pages 1877–1901. Curran Associates, Inc.

Jacob Devlin, Ming-Wei Chang, Kenton Lee, and Kristina Toutanova. 2019. BERT: Pre-training of deep bidirectional transformers for language understanding. In *Proceedings of the 2019 Conference of the North American Chapter of the Association for Computational Linguistics: Human Language Technologies, Volume 1 (Long and Short Papers)*, pages 4171–4186, Minneapolis, Minnesota. Association for Computational Linguistics.

Alexander Fabbri, Patrick Ng, Zhiguo Wang, Ramesh Nallapati, and Bing Xiang. 2020. Template-based question generation from retrieved sentences for improved unsupervised question answering. In *Proceedings of the 58th Annual Meeting of the Association for Computational Linguistics*, pages 4508–4513, Online. Association for Computational Linguistics.

Michael Heilman and Noah A Smith. 2009. Question generation via overgenerating transformations and ranking. Technical report, Carnegie-Mellon University.

Joel Jang, Seonghyeon Ye, and Minjoon Seo. 2022. Can large language models truly understand prompts? a case study with negated prompts.

Melvin Johnson, Mike Schuster, Quoc V. Le, Maxim Krikun, Yonghui Wu, Zhifeng Chen, Nikhil Thorat, Fernanda Viégas, Martin Wattenberg, Greg Corrado, Macduff Hughes, and Jeffrey Dean. 2017. Google's multilingual neural machine translation system: Enabling zero-shot translation. *Transactions of the Association for Computational Linguistics*, 5:339–351.

Huiyuan Lai, Antonio Toral, and Malvina Nissim. 2021. Thank you BART! rewarding pre-trained models improves formality style transfer. In *Proceedings of the 59th Annual Meeting of the Association for Computational Linguistics and the 11th International Joint Conference on Natural Language Processing (Volume 2: Short Papers)*, pages 484–494, Online. Association for Computational Linguistics.

Mike Lewis and Angela Fan. 2019. Generative question answering: Learning to answer the whole question. In *International Conference on Learning Representations*.

Mike Lewis, Yinhan Liu, Naman Goyal, Marjan Ghazvininejad, Abdelrahman Mohamed, Omer Levy, Veselin Stoyanov, and Luke Zettlemoyer. 2020. BART: Denoising sequence-to-sequence pre-training for natural language generation, translation, and comprehension. In *Proceedings of the 58th Annual Meeting of the Association for Computational Linguistics*, pages 7871–7880, Online. Association for Computational Linguistics.

Patrick Lewis, Yuxiang Wu, Linqing Liu, Pasquale Minervini, Heinrich Küttler, Aleksandra Piktus, Pontus Stenetorp, and Sebastian Riedel. 2021. PAQ: 65 million probably-asked questions and what you can do with them. *Transactions of the Association for Computational Linguistics*, 9:1098–1115.

Pengfei Liu, Weizhe Yuan, Jinlan Fu, Zhengbao Jiang, Hiroaki Hayashi, and Graham Neubig. 2021. Pretrain, prompt, and predict: A systematic survey of prompting methods in natural language processing. *CoRR*, abs/2107.13586.

Yinhan Liu, Myle Ott, Naman Goyal, Jingfei Du, Mandar Joshi, Danqi Chen, Omer Levy, Mike Lewis, Luke Zettlemoyer, and Veselin Stoyanov. 2019. Roberta: A robustly optimized BERT pretraining approach. *CoRR*, abs/1907.11692.

Daniel Loureiro, Aminette D'Souza, Areej Nasser Muhajab, Isabella A. White, Gabriel Wong, Luis Espinosa Anke, Leonardo Neves, Francesco Barbieri, and Jose Camacho-Collados. 2022. Tempowic: An evaluation benchmark for detecting meaning shift in social media.

Daniel Loureiro, Kiamehr Rezaee, Mohammad Taher Pilehvar, and Jose Camacho-Collados. 2021. Analysis and Evaluation of Language Models for Word Sense Disambiguation. *Computational Linguistics*, 47(2):387–443.

Chenyang Lyu, Lifeng Shang, Yvette Graham, Jennifer Foster, Xin Jiang, and Qun Liu. 2021. Improving unsupervised question answering via summarization-informed question generation. In *Proceedings of the 2021 Conference on Empirical Methods in Natural Language Processing*, pages 4134–4148, Online and Punta Cana, Dominican Republic. Association for Computational Linguistics.

Sewon Min, Xinxi Lyu, Ari Holtzman, Mikel Artetxe, Mike Lewis, Hannaneh Hajishirzi, and Luke Zettlemoyer. 2022. Rethinking the role of demonstrations: What makes in-context learning work? *arXiv preprint arXiv:2202.12837*.

Alec Radford, Jeff Wu, Rewon Child, David Luan, Dario Amodei, and Ilya Sutskever. 2019. Language models are unsupervised multitask learners.

Ilya Sutskever, Oriol Vinyals, and Quoc V Le. 2014. Sequence to sequence learning with neural networks. In *Advances in Neural Information Processing Systems*, volume 27. Curran Associates, Inc.

Thomas Wolf, Lysandre Debut, Victor Sanh, Julien Chaumond, Clement Delangue, Anthony Moi, Pierric Cistac, Tim Rault, Remi Louf, Morgan Funtowicz, Joe Davison, Sam Shleifer, Patrick von Platen, Clara Ma, Yacine Jernite, Julien Plu, Canwen Xu, Teven Le Scao, Sylvain Gugger, Mariama Drame, Quentin Lhoest, and Alexander Rush. 2020. Transformers: State-of-the-art natural language processing. In *Proceedings of the 2020 Conference on Empirical Methods in Natural Language Processing: System Demonstrations*, pages 38–45, Online. Association for Computational Linguistics.

Zhilin Yang, Zihang Dai, Yiming Yang, Jaime Carbonell, Russ R Salakhutdinov, and Quoc V Le. 2019. Xlnet: Generalized autoregressive pretraining for language understanding. *Advances in neural information processing systems*, 32.

Yongxin Zhou, François Portet, and Fabien Ringeval. 2022. Effectiveness of French language models on abstractive dialogue summarization task. In *Proceedings of the Thirteenth Language Resources and Evaluation Conference*, pages 3571–3581, Marseille, France. European Language Resources Association.

Using Deep Mixture-of-Experts to Detect Word Meaning Shift for TempoWiC

Ze Chen, Kangxu Wang, Zijian Cai, Jiewen Zheng Jiarong He, Max Gao Jason Zhang
Interactive Entertainment Group of Netease Inc., Guangzhou, China
{jackchen,wangkangxu,caizijian01,zhengjiewen,gzhejiarong,jgao, fyzhang}@corp.netease.com

Abstract

This paper mainly describes the *dma* submission to the TempoWiC task, which achieves a macro-F1 score of 77.05% and attains the first place in this task. We first explore the impact of different pre-trained language models. Then we adopt data cleaning, data augmentation, and adversarial training strategies to enhance the model generalization and robustness. For further improvement, we integrate POS information and word semantic representation using a Mixture-of-Experts (MoE) approach. The experimental results show that MoE can overcome the feature overuse issue and combine the context, POS, and word semantic features well. Additionally, we use a model ensemble method for the final prediction, which has been proven effective by many research works.

1 Introduction

Lexical Semantic Change (LSC) Detection has drawn increasing attention in the past years(Liu et al., 2021; Laicher et al., 2021). Existed research works (Liu et al., 2021) have shown that contextual word embeddings such as those produced by BERT (Devlin et al., 2018) have great advantages over non-contextual embeddings for inferring semantic shift when there is limited data. Meanwhile, many datasets are released to accelerate research in this direction. Pilehvar and Camacho-Collados (2018) proposed Word-in-Context (WiC) dataset as an benchmark for generic evaluation of context-sensitive representations. Raganato et al. (2020) extended WiC to XL-WiC dataset with multilingual extensions. In contrast to these, TempoWiC (Loureiro et al., 2022b) is crucially designed around the time-sensitive meaning shift and instances of word usage tied to Twitter trending topics. Our main work is to build a system that can detect semantic changes of target words in tweet pairs during different time periods for TempoWiC. It is framed as a binary classification task that addresses whether two instances of a target word have the same meaning. And pre-trained language models are adopted to produce contextual embeddings.

2 Background

2.1 Task Description

TempoWiC (Loureiro et al., 2022b) is a new benchmark especially aimed at detecting a meaning shift in social media. Given a pair of sentences and a target word, the task is framed as a simple binary classification problem in deciding whether the meaning corresponding to the first target word in context is the same as the second one or not.

The dataset of TempoWiC consists of 3297 annotated instances, which are divided into train/dev/test sets of size 1,428/396/1,473 instances, respectively. The target words involved in this task do not overlap between sets. For each sample, tweet pairs containing the target word were collected from the Twitter API at different time periods. The prior date is exactly one year before the peak date to avoid seasonal confound factors. The label True indicates that the word has the same meaning in the two tweets, while the label False indicates that the meaning is different.

2.2 Pre-trained Language Models

Recently, pre-trained language models (LM) have achieved remarkable achievement on natural language processing tasks, becoming one of the most effective methods for engineers and scholars. Transformers-based Pre-trained language models such as BERT(Devlin et al., 2018), RoBERTa(Liu et al., 2019), DeBERTa(He et al., 2020), DeBERTaV3(He et al., 2021) is designed to pre-trained deep representation from unlabeled text, which can be fine-tuned with just one additional output layer to create state-of-the-art models for a wide range of tasks, such as question answering and language inference, without substantial task-specific architecture modifications.

Proceedings of the The First Workshop on Ever Evolving NLP (EvoNLP), pages 7 - 11
December 7, 2022

By training language models using Twitter corpora from different time periods, (Loureiro et al., 2022a) showed that language undergoes semantic transformations over time, proving that training a language model with outdated corpora leads to a decline in performance.

2.3 Mixture-of-Experts

MoE (Arnaud et al., 2019) is an approach for conditionally computing a representation. Given several expert inputs, the output of MoE is a weighted combination of the experts. Recently, MoE achieves significant improvements on several natural language processing tasks, such as named entity recognition (Meng et al., 2021), recommendation(Zhu et al., 2020) and machine translation(Shazeer et al., 2017).

3 System Overview

In this section, we first present the framework details for the models adopted in our work. Then we introduce several strategies for improving the models' robustness. Finally, we talk about the design of the model ensemble method.

3.1 Models

Our model framework can be divided into three layers:*encoding*, *matching* and *prediction*. The *encoding* layer is meant for sequence modeling to capture contextual semantic representation. The *matching* layer focuses on finding out the interrelation and differences between the target words in two different tweets. And the *prediction* layer is implemented as a classifier that decides whether the meaning of the target word is the same or not.

A. Base Model Figure 1 shows the details of our base model. Two tweets are concatenated together and fed into a pre-trained LM, and the contextual embeddings(e.g. E_1, E_2 [1]) corresponding to the target word on each tweet of the pair can be achieved. Then E_1 and E_2 are processed by the *matching* layer to find the difference in these two tweets. The procedure can be summarized as follows:

$$E_{match} = [E_1; E_2; E_1 - E_2; E_1 * E_2; E_{CLS}]$$

$$y_o = softmax(MLP(E_{match}))$$

$$loss = CrossEntropy(y_o, y_{true})$$

where E_{CLS} is the embedding of the first token, E_{match} is the output of the *matching* layer, MLP is a multi-layer perceptron, y_{true} is the gold label and y_o is the output by the base model. $E_1 * E_2$ means the Hadamard product of these two vectors, and $E_1 - E_2$ represents the elementwise subtraction.

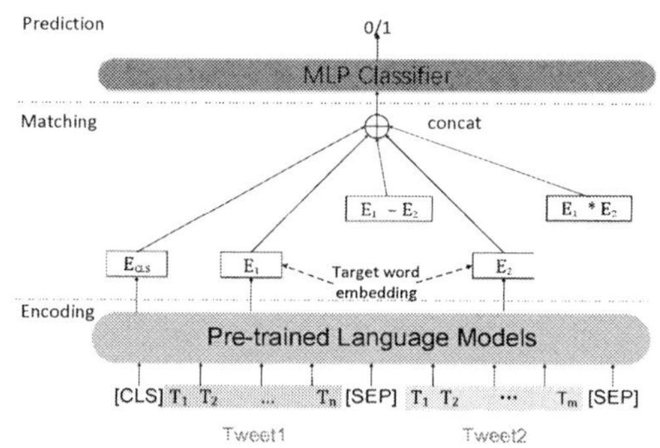

Figure 1: Base Model Architecture

B. MoE Models Figure 2 gives a glimpse of our MoE-based model architecture. We extend the base model with two separate BiLSTM to integrate the POS information and the word semantic representation. For a pair of tweets, we first extract the contextual embeddings for the target word from pre-trained LM, and then we use two separate BiLSTM to get POS encoding and word semantic encoding. At last, an MoE module is adopted to merge these three encodings for the target word. The generated embeddings(e.g. $E_1^{'}$, $E_2^{'}$) for the target word are then processed by the *matching* layer and *prediction* layer as described above. Here we denote the POS encoding for the target word in the pair of tweets as E_1^P, E_2^P, and denote the GloVe-initialized word semantic encoding as E_1^G, E_2^G respectively.

The details of an MoE module for this task are given in Figure 3, which consists of a gating network and three experts. The procedure can be summarized as follows:

$$w_C, w_P, w_G = Gate(E_1, E_1^P, E_1^G)$$

$$E_1^{'} = w_C * E_1 + w_P * E_1^P + w_G * E_1^G$$

where w_C, w_P, w_G are the weights for contextual expert, POS expert, and word semantic expert respectively, $Gate$ stands for the gating network, and

[1] We experimented with different target word representations: the first token in the word span, the mean value of all tokens in the span, the concatenation of the first token and last token in the span. And we found that adopting the concatenation of the first token and last token in the span can perform better than others. Please refer to Appendix A for more details.

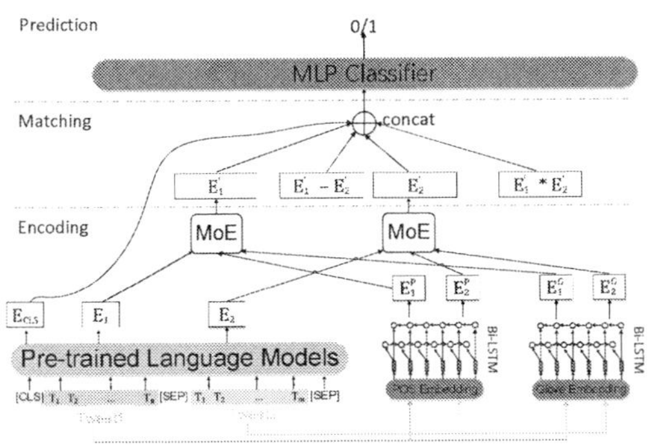

Figure 2: MoE-based Model Architecture

$E_1^{'}$ is the output of MoE module for the target word in the first tweet. We can get $E_2^{'}$ for the target word in the second tweet by the same approach. And two gating networks are implemented here.

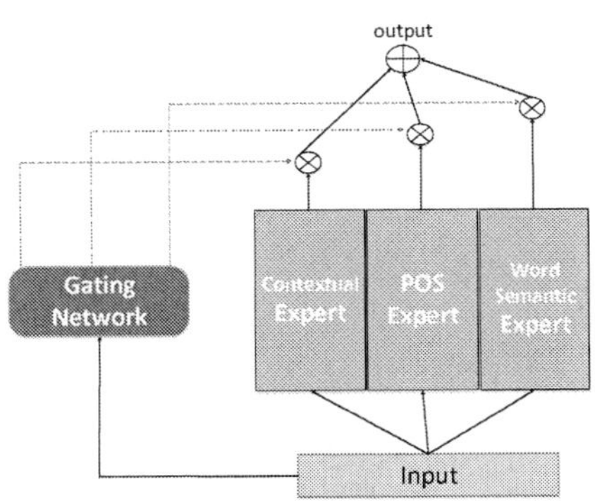

Figure 3: Illustration of an MoE module

- **Separate Gating Network(S-Gate):** The weight for each expert is calculated separately. We define a task-specific vector V_t, the weight for expert i can be calculated as: $w_i = \sigma(\theta[V_t, E^i])$, where θ are trainable parameters, $[,]$ is the concatenation and σ is the Sigmoid activation, E^i is the encoding of i-th expert.
- **Joint Gating Network(J-Gate):** The weights for all experts are calculated together. We define the weight vector for all experts as W, which is a three-dimension vector and can be calculated as: $W = softmax(\theta[E^1, E^2, E^3])$, where θ are trainable parameters.

3.2 Data Cleaning and Augmentation

Given that the dataset is somewhat small, and there are some flaws in the labeled data, we adopt simple cleaning and augmentation strategies. We simply remove HTML tags and emojis in tweets, and replace the symbol *@username* with a generic placeholder. Moreover, we directly remove the wrongly labeled samples of the target word position. There are many different data augmentation strategies: token shuffling, cutoff, back-translation, and so on. We just introduce the WiC dataset(Pilehvar and Camacho-Collados, 2018) for data augmentation in this paper.

3.3 Adversarial Training

Adversarial attack has been well applied in both computer vision and natural language processing to improve the model's robustness. We implement this strategy with Fast Gradient Method(Goodfellow et al., 2014), which directly uses the gradient to compute the perturbation and augments the input with this perturbation to maximizes the adversarial loss. The training procedure can be summarized as follows:

$$\min_{\theta} E_{(x,y)\sim\mathcal{D}}[\max_{\Delta x \in \Omega} L(x + \Delta x, y; \theta)]$$

where x is input, y is the gold label, $\mathcal{D}$ is the dataset, θ is the model parameters, $L(x + \Delta x, y; \theta)$ is the loss function and Δx is the perturbation.

3.4 Model Ensemble

For the final prediction, we implement a model ensemble method. In detail, we use one base model and the other two MoE models mentioned above to get the prediction scores and then average these output scores as the final result.

4 Experiments

4.1 Experimental Setup

Our implementation is based on the Transformers library by HuggingFace(Wolf et al., 2019) for the pre-trained models and corresponding tokenizers. During training, the data is processed by batches of size 8, the maximum length of each sample is set to 256, and the learning rate is set to 1e-6 with a warmup ratio over 10%. By default, we set ϵ to 1.0 in FGM and set the MLP to two layers with a hidden size of 256.

When MoE models are employed, the hidden size of BiLSTM is set to 1024, and the pre-trained Twitter GloVe word vectors [2] are used for word embedding initialization. Moreover, we use nltk

[2] `https://nlp.stanford.edu/projects/glove/`

toolkit [3] to extract POS tags, and the POS embeddings are randomly initialized. Our system jointly optimizes over different experts, but their model architectures differ. We adopt differential learning rates to tackle this problem. The learning rate for the transformer-based model is set to 1e-6, and the learning rate for BiLSTM is set to 1e-4.

4.2 Results and Analysis

In this section, we first present experimental results on the base model. Then we experiment with MoE models using the effective strategies validated on the base model. At last, the results of the model ensemble are reported.

We explore the impact of different pre-trained LMs adopted as the contextual encoder. Results given in Table 1 show that DeBERTa-large can perform well on this task. And TimeLMs(Loureiro et al., 2022a) can perform better than generic RoBERTa since they are implemented and adapted to the Twitter domain. Moreover, TimeLMs-2020-09 can achieve almost the best results among TimeLMs, largely because the dev dataset is distributed over this time period. From the last two rows in Table 1, we can find that data cleaning and augmentation can increase the macro-F1 score by 2.83 percentage points, and FGM training can increase this indicator by 2.57%. Additionally, the ablation study results on *matching* layer are presented in Appendix A, we can find that the first token $[CLS]$ embedding can help improve the performance of this task. The subtraction and Hadamard product operations can also help find the difference between target words in two tweets.

When we experiment with MoE models, the data cleaning and augmentation, and FGM training are adopted by default. And the pre-trained DeBERTa-large is used for the contextual encoder. Table 2 shows the performance of different MoE models. We can find that when integrating POS information and word semantic representation by using an MoE architecture, the performance can improve a lot. More specifically, the MoE model with S-Gate and J-Gate can achieve macro-F1 scores of 79.25% and 79.19% respectively, both of which increase the base by more than 2%. For further analysis, ablation studies are done here. We experiment with POS information and GloVe separately and find that using an MoE model to integrate POS information can improve the performance by 1%, while using an MoE model to combine word semantic representation can increase the macro-F1 score by about 2%.

Model	Accuracy	macro-F1
TimeLMs-2019-12	67.17%	63.34%
TimeLMs-2020-03	68.18%	65.20%
TimeLMs-2020-09	68.43%	65.42%
TimeLMs-2020-12	68.18%	65.20%
TimeLMs-2021-03	66.67%	63.88%
TimeLMs-2022-03	68.18%	65.12%
RoBERTa-base	61.62%	60.30%
DeBERTa-base	69.90%	65.60%
DeBERTa-large	71.72%	71.68%
+ Data Aug	74.63%	74.51%
+ Data Aug + FGM(Base)	**77.53%**	**77.08%**

Table 1: Results of base model on dev dataset

Model	Accuracy	macro-F1
Base	77.53%	77.08%
S-Gate + POS + GloVe	**79.29%**	**79.25%**
S-Gate + POS	78.26%	77.20%
S-Gate + GloVe	78.19%	77.18%
J-Gate + POS + GloVe	**79.29%**	79.19%
J-Gate + POS	78.62%	78.31%
J-Gate + GloVe	77.55%	77.12%

Table 2: Results of MoE-based models on dev dataset

Table 3 gives the results of our model ensemble method. By averaging the prediction scores of one base model and the other two MoE models(S-Gate + POS + GloVe, J-Gate + POS + GloVe), the macro-F1 score can increase by more than 1% on the dev dataset. And our model ensemble method achieves a macro-F1 score of 77.05% on the test dataset, which attains the first place in this task.

Dataset	Accuracy	macro-F1
Dev	80.81%	80.5%
Test	**78.34%**	**77.05%**

Table 3: Ensemble results on both Dev and Test dataset

5 Conclusion

In this work, we provide an overview of the combined approach to detect the meaning shift in social media. We investigate the impact of adopting different pre-trained LMs, finding that DeBERTa performs best for this task. Experimental results show that strategies such as data augmentation and adversarial training can enhance the model's robustness. In particular, incorporating POS information and word-level semantic representation with MoE models can significantly improve performance. For future work, we will investigate how to incorporate different TimeLMs with MoE models for this task.

[3] https://www.nltk.org/

References

Estephe Arnaud, Arnaud Dapogny, and Kevin Bailly. 2019. Tree-gated deep mixture-of-experts for pose-robust face alignment.

Jacob Devlin, Ming-Wei Chang, Kenton Lee, and Kristina Toutanova. 2018. Bert: Pre-training of deep bidirectional transformers for language understanding. *arXiv preprint arXiv:1810.04805*.

Ian J Goodfellow, Jonathon Shlens, and Christian Szegedy. 2014. Explaining and harnessing adversarial examples. *arXiv preprint arXiv:1412.6572*.

Pengcheng He, Jianfeng Gao, and Weizhu Chen. 2021. Debertav3: Improving deberta using electra-style pre-training with gradient-disentangled embedding sharing. *arXiv preprint arXiv:2111.09543*.

Pengcheng He, Xiaodong Liu, Jianfeng Gao, and Weizhu Chen. 2020. Deberta: Decoding-enhanced bert with disentangled attention. *arXiv preprint arXiv:2006.03654*.

Severin Laicher, Sinan Kurtyigit, Dominik Schlechtweg, Jonas Kuhn, and Sabine Schulte im Walde. 2021. Explaining and improving bert performance on lexical semantic change detection. *arXiv preprint arXiv:2103.07259*.

Yang Liu, Alan Medlar, and Dorota Glowacka. 2021. Statistically significant detection of semantic shifts using contextual word embeddings. In *Proceedings of the 2nd Workshop on Evaluation and Comparison of NLP Systems*, pages 104–113, Punta Cana, Dominican Republic. Association for Computational Linguistics.

Yinhan Liu, Myle Ott, Naman Goyal, Jingfei Du, Mandar Joshi, Danqi Chen, Omer Levy, Mike Lewis, Luke Zettlemoyer, and Veselin Stoyanov. 2019. Roberta: A robustly optimized bert pretraining approach. *arXiv preprint arXiv:1907.11692*.

Daniel Loureiro, Francesco Barbieri, Leonardo Neves, Luis Espinosa Anke, and Jose Camacho-collados. 2022a. TimeLMs: Diachronic language models from Twitter. In *Proceedings of the 60th Annual Meeting of the Association for Computational Linguistics: System Demonstrations*, pages 251–260, Dublin, Ireland. Association for Computational Linguistics.

Daniel Loureiro, Aminette D'Souza, Areej Nasser Muhajab, Isabella A. White, Gabriel Wong, Luis Espinosa Anke, Leonardo Neves, Francesco Barbieri, and Jose Camacho-Collados. 2022b. Tempowic: An evaluation benchmark for detecting meaning shift in social media.

Tao Meng, Anjie Fang, Oleg Rokhlenko, and Shervin Malmasi. 2021. Gemnet: Effective gated gazetteer representations for recognizing complex entities in low-context input. In *Proceedings of the 2021 Conference of the North American Chapter of the Association for Computational Linguistics: Human Language Technologies*, pages 1499–1512.

Mohammad Taher Pilehvar and Jose Camacho-Collados. 2018. Wic: the word-in-context dataset for evaluating context-sensitive meaning representations. *arXiv preprint arXiv:1808.09121*.

Alessandro Raganato, Tommaso Pasini, Jose Camacho-Collados, and Mohammad Taher Pilehvar. 2020. XL-WiC: A multilingual benchmark for evaluating semantic contextualization. In *Proceedings of the 2020 Conference on Empirical Methods in Natural Language Processing (EMNLP)*, pages 7193–7206, Online. Association for Computational Linguistics.

Noam Shazeer, Azalia Mirhoseini, Krzysztof Maziarz, Andy Davis, Quoc Le, Geoffrey Hinton, and Jeff Dean. 2017. Outrageously large neural networks: The sparsely-gated mixture-of-experts layer. *arXiv preprint arXiv:1701.06538*.

Thomas Wolf, Lysandre Debut, Victor Sanh, Julien Chaumond, Clement Delangue, Anthony Moi, Pierric Cistac, Tim Rault, Rémi Louf, Morgan Funtowicz, et al. 2019. Huggingface's transformers: State-of-the-art natural language processing. *arXiv preprint arXiv:1910.03771*.

Ziwei Zhu, Shahin Sefati, Parsa Saadatpanah, and James Caverlee. 2020. Recommendation for new users and new items via randomized training and mixture-of-experts transformation. In *Proceedings of the 43rd International ACM SIGIR Conference on Research and Development in Information Retrieval*, pages 1121–1130.

A Additional Experiments on the base model

In this part, we present several additional experimental results on the base model.

We tried different target word representation methods for contextual embedding. The results on dev dataset are listed in Table 4.

Target word	Accuracy	macro-F1
$First$	75.6%	74.49%
$Mean$	74.94%	74.46%
$First + Last$	**77.53%**	**77.08%**

Table 4: Results of different target word representation methods

To make further analysis, we conducted ablation studies to investigate the contribution of different components of *matching* layer. Results are shown in Table 5.

Matching layer	Accuracy	macro-F1
$E_1 + E_2$	75.92%	74.74%
$+ E_{CLS}$	77.15%	76.45%
$+ E_{CLS} + [E_1 - E_2] + [E_1 * E_2]$	**77.53%**	**77.08%**

Table 5: Results of different components of *matching* layer

Using Two Losses and Two Datasets Simultaneously to Improve TempoWiC Accuracy

Mohammad Javad Pirhadi, Motahhare Mirzaei and **Sauleh Eetemadi**
Iran University of Science and Technology at Tehran, Iran
{mohammad_pirhadi, m_mirzaei96}@comp.iust.ac.ir, sauleh@iust.ac.ir

Abstract

WSD (Word Sense Disambiguation) is the task of identifying which sense of a word is meant in a sentence or other segment of text. Researchers have worked on this task (e.g. Pustejovsky, 2002) for years but it's still a challenging one even for SOTA (state-of-the-art) LMs (language models). The new dataset, TempoWiC introduced by Loureiro et al. (2022b) focuses on the fact that words change over time. Their best baseline achieves 70.33% macro-F1. In this work, we use two different losses simultaneously to train RoBERTa-based classification models. We also improve our model by using another similar dataset to generalize better. Our best configuration beats their best baseline by 4.23% and reaches 74.56% macro-F1.

1 Introduction

In 2019, Pilehvar and Camacho-Collados (2018) introduced WiC dataset. It is framed as a binary classification task between pairs of sentences including one identical target word with different meanings. In 2020, XL-WiC was introduced by Raganato et al. (2020) and made WiC richer by providing more examples and adding more languages. We benefit from the English part of XL-WiC as a helping dataset to improve the generalization of our model.

Loureiro et al. (2022b) baselines include: RoBERTa (Liu et al., 2019) base and large, TimeLMs (Loureiro et al., 2022a) 2019-90M and 2021-124M and BERTweet (Nguyen et al., 2020) base and large. They examine two different methods of using these models: Fine-tuning and SP-WSD layer pooling weights as explained in Loureiro et al. (2022c). The best result is for TimeLMs-2019-90M with SP-WSD with 70.33% macro-F1. We examine RoBERTa-base and TimeLMs-Jun2022-153M.

For classification, many previous works (e.g. Peters et al., 2019) use standard practice and concatenate both sentences with a `[SEP]` token and fine-tune the `[CLS]` embedding. In this work, we use two different losses simultaneously, cross entropy loss on RoBERTa classification head output as standard practice and add cosine embedding loss on average of target word output embeddings.

2 Methodology

2.1 Model

We use LMs as base model. We add classification head and also cosine similarity + sigmoid on top of them. The classification head consists of two FC (fully connected) layers and a dropout layer between them (like standard RoBERTa classification head). RoBERTa uses a byte-level BPE (Byte-Pair Encoding) encoding scheme so it's possible that we have multiple embeddings for a single word. For second output path, we average embeddings (it can be more than one as explained) related to target word in first sentence and second sentence and compare them using cosine similarity, finally we apply sigmoid activation to get a binary classification. Our experiments shows that the second output path is more accurate by a large margin. Figure 1 shows an overview of described architecture.

2.2 Loss Function

For the loss function, we have the sum of two losses, one on standard RoBERTa classification head and another on similarity (in case of the same meaning) or dissimilarity (in case of the different meaning) of the embeddings of the last layer related to the target word. For the former, we use cross entropy loss and for latter we use cosine embedding loss. The second loss, help our model to make similar contextual embeddings for target word closer and push dissimilar ones away from each other.

Proceedings of the The First Workshop on Ever Evolving NLP (EvoNLP), pages 12 - 15
December 7, 2022 ©2022 Association for Computational Linguistics

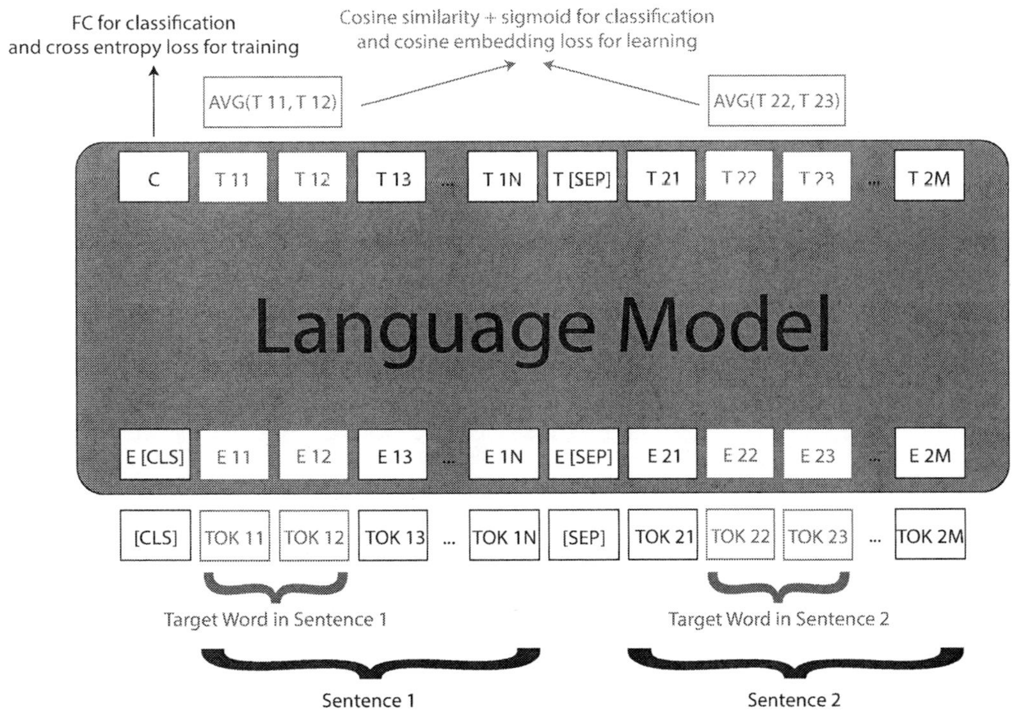

Figure 1: An overview of architecture. We use two losses simultaneously. First one is cross entropy loss on standard classifier head (black path) and the second one is cosine embedding loss on average of target word output embeddings (red path).

2.3 Dataset

The main dataset is TempoWiC, but we also use the XL-WiC dataset to make our model more robust. It's important to know that XL-WiC samples are not tweets so it is out-of-domain data and the added data may cause model accuracy to degrade if the combined dataset is not representative. We explored using the main dataset without adding any sample from the XL-WiC dataset, by adding a random subset of XL-WiC, and also by adding the whole XL-WiC.

2.4 Framework & Tools

We use PyTorch (Paszke et al., 2019) + HuggingFace transformers (Wolf et al., 2020) to implement our models and for reporting results we use the Codalab online platform[1].

2.5 Hyper-parameters

We use Ray Tune (Liaw et al., 2018) to tune our hyper-parameters including learning rate, train epochs, random seed, batch size and weight decay. Increasing weight decay helps us avoid over-fitting which was the main problem in our initial model.

[1] `https://codalab.lisn.upsaclay.fr/competitions/5360`

3 Experiments

We have multiple configurations to test:

1. Model
    - RoBERTa-base
    - TimeLMs-Jun2022-153M
2. Output
    - Standard Classifier Head (FC)
    - Cosine Similarity + Sigmoid (CS+S)
3. How we use XL-WiC
    - Do not use (No)
    - A subset as described (Sub)
    - Whole XL-WiC (All)

3.1 Results

The biggest problem we were facing was over-fitting. This is expected since we use transformer-based LMs.

Output	Model	XL-WiC Use	Macro-F1
Classifier	RoBERTa-base	No	62.35%
		Sub	65.98%
		All	63.56%
	TimeLMs-Jun2022-153M	No	64.54%
		Sub	73.16%
		All	72.77%
Similarity	RoBERTa-base	No	67.26%
		Sub	68.29%
		All	67.29%
	TimeLMs-Jun2022-153M	No	66.69%
		Sub	**74.56%**
		All	72.32%
Official Baselines	TimeLMs-2019-90M-SIM	No	70.33%
	RoBERTa-L-SIM	No	67.09%
	RoBERTa-L-FT	No	59.10%
	TimeLMs-2019-90M-FT	No	57.70%
	Random	No	50.00%
	All True	No	26.79%

Table 1: All results are obtained from the Codalab online platform on Tempo-WiC test set.

The most accurate configuration is TimeLMs-Jun2022-153M with cosine similarity + sigmoid output trained on TempoWiC and a subset of XL-WiC. In the following paragraphs, we are going to analysis the results.

First, the results show that TimeLMs-Jun2022-153M beats RoBERTa in all possible configurations, the reason is simple: TempoWiC consists of tweets and TimeLMs-Jun2022-153M is trained on tweets too, but RoBERTa is not trained on tweets.

Second, using XL-WiC improves results in all cases. Using all XL-WiC example reduces the accuracy because the distribution is different (the samples are not tweets) and it has almost $4\times$ data in comparison to TempoWiC. If we use all of its data, we can not expect better accuracy because the training set distribution will be different from the test distribution.

Last, the cosine similarity + sigmoid output is better in most cases in comparison to the standard classifier head. We think it's because of more focus on the target word embedding in comparison to more focus on the whole context.

4 Future Work

In the future work, more configurations can be explored:

1. Selecting the subset of XL-WiC more wisely, instead of randomly selecting. For example, considering the maximum possible use of unique words.

2. Using more layers to calculate similarity, instead of using only the last layer. For example, the sum of the last 4 layers is another common choice in word sense disambiguation settings.

3. Exploring more similarity functions, instead of cosine similarity. For example, euclidean distance can also be explored.

5 Conclusion

In this work, we beat the best baseline of Loureiro et al. (2022b) by a large margin. To do this we use two losses simultaneously (standard classifier head cross entropy loss and cosine embedding loss on average of target word output embeddings) to train SOTA LMs, and also use XL-WiC as a helping dataset to generalize better. The best LM was TimeLMs-Jun2022-153M which is a pre-trained model on 153M tweets.

6 Acknowledgements

We would like to express our special thanks of gratitude to Mohammad Mahdi Javid who helped us with preparing training resources.

References

Richard Liaw, Eric Liang, Robert Nishihara, Philipp Moritz, Joseph E. Gonzalez, and Ion Stoica. 2018. Tune: A research platform for distributed model selection and training.

Yinhan Liu, Myle Ott, Naman Goyal, Jingfei Du, Mandar Joshi, Danqi Chen, Omer Levy, Mike Lewis, Luke Zettlemoyer, and Veselin Stoyanov. 2019. Roberta: A robustly optimized BERT pretraining approach. *CoRR*, abs/1907.11692.

Daniel Loureiro, Francesco Barbieri, Leonardo Neves, Luis Espinosa Anke, and Jose Camacho-collados. 2022a. TimeLMs: Diachronic language models from Twitter. In *Proceedings of the 60th Annual Meeting of the Association for Computational Linguistics: System Demonstrations*, pages 251–260, Dublin, Ireland. Association for Computational Linguistics.

Daniel Loureiro, Aminette D'Souza, Areej Nasser Muhajab, Isabella A. White, Gabriel Wong, Luis Espinosa-Anke, Leonardo Neves, Francesco Barbieri, and Jose Camacho-Collados. 2022b. TempoWiC: An evaluation benchmark for detecting meaning shift in social media. In *Proceedings of the 29th International Conference on Computational Linguistics*, pages 3353–3359, Gyeongju, Republic of Korea. International Committee on Computational Linguistics.

Daniel Loureiro, Alípio Mário Jorge, and Jose Camacho-Collados. 2022c. Lmms reloaded: Transformer-based sense embeddings for disambiguation and beyond. *Artificial Intelligence*, 305:103661.

Dat Quoc Nguyen, Thanh Vu, and Anh Tuan Nguyen. 2020. BERTweet: A pre-trained language model for English tweets. In *Proceedings of the 2020 Conference on Empirical Methods in Natural Language Processing: System Demonstrations*, pages 9–14, Online. Association for Computational Linguistics.

Adam Paszke, Sam Gross, Francisco Massa, Adam Lerer, James Bradbury, Gregory Chanan, Trevor Killeen, Zeming Lin, Natalia Gimelshein, Luca Antiga, Alban Desmaison, Andreas Kopf, Edward Yang, Zachary DeVito, Martin Raison, Alykhan Tejani, Sasank Chilamkurthy, Benoit Steiner, Lu Fang, Junjie Bai, and Soumith Chintala. 2019. Pytorch: An imperative style, high-performance deep learning library. In H. Wallach, H. Larochelle, A. Beygelzimer, F. d'Alché-Buc, E. Fox, and R. Garnett, editors, *Advances in Neural Information Processing Systems 32*, pages 8024–8035. Curran Associates, Inc.

Matthew E. Peters, Mark Neumann, Robert L. Logan IV, Roy Schwartz, Vidur Joshi, Sameer Singh, and Noah A. Smith. 2019. Knowledge enhanced contextual word representations. *CoRR*, abs/1909.04164.

Mohammad Taher Pilehvar and José Camacho-Collados. 2018. Wic: 10, 000 example pairs for evaluating context-sensitive representations. *CoRR*, abs/1808.09121.

James Pustejovsky. 2002. The generative lexicon. *Computational Linguistics*, 17.

Alessandro Raganato, Tommaso Pasini, José Camacho-Collados, and Mohammad Taher Pilehvar. 2020. Xl-wic: A multilingual benchmark for evaluating semantic contextualization. *CoRR*, abs/2010.06478.

Thomas Wolf, Lysandre Debut, Victor Sanh, Julien Chaumond, Clement Delangue, Anthony Moi, Pierric Cistac, Tim Rault, Remi Louf, Morgan Funtowicz, Joe Davison, Sam Shleifer, Patrick von Platen, Clara Ma, Yacine Jernite, Julien Plu, Canwen Xu, Teven Le Scao, Sylvain Gugger, Mariama Drame, Quentin Lhoest, and Alexander Rush. 2020. Transformers: State-of-the-art natural language processing. In *Proceedings of the 2020 Conference on Empirical Methods in Natural Language Processing: System Demonstrations*, pages 38–45, Online. Association for Computational Linguistics.

Class Incremental Learning for Intent Classification with Limited or No Old Data

Debjit Paul[*]
EPFL
debjit.paul@epfl.ch

Daniil Sorokin
Amazon Alexa AI
dsorokin@amazon.de

Judith Gaspers
Amazon Alexa AI
gaspers@amazon.de

Abstract

In this paper, we explore class-incremental learning for intent classification (IC) in a setting with limited old data available. IC is the task of mapping user utterances to their corresponding intents. Even though class-incremental learning without storing the old data yields high potential of reducing human and computational resources in industry NLP model releases, to the best of our knowledge, it hasn't been studied for NLP classification tasks in the literature before. In this work, we compare several contemporary class-incremental learning methods, i.e., BERT warm start, L2, Elastic Weight Consolidation, RecAdam and Knowledge Distillation within two realistic class-incremental learning scenarios: one where only the previous model is assumed to be available, but no data corresponding to old classes, and one in which limited unlabeled data for old classes is assumed to be available. Our results indicate that among the investigated continual learning methods, Knowledge Distillation worked best for our class-incremental learning tasks, and adding limited unlabeled data helps the model in both adaptability and stability.

1 Introduction

In real-world scenarios, NLP models are regularly updated to incorporate new functionality that either covers new data distributions or includes new output classes (Diethe et al., 2018). We focus on the latter scenario in this work, and we consider a feature expansion use case for a spoken language understanding (SLU) task in a voice assistant, such as Siri or Alexa. In particular, we focus on the task of intent classification (IC), which is a common sub-task in SLU that aims to map an input user utterance to an intent supported by the system (for instance, PLAYMUSIC for *play the best songs from Madonna*). With feature expansion, new intents are to be added to the SLU model over time to support new output classes that corresponds to new user-facing features in a voice assistant.

A regular feature expansion process in production results in a series of consecutive SLU model releases that are trained for the same intent classification task, in which new output classes are being added to the model. Having regular model releases, it is wasteful of computing and human resources to start from scratch every time and not re-use the previous release model in one form or another. Moreover, as our research community moves towards building NLP systems that are environmentally friendly (e.g., requiring less training time and computational resources), class incremental learning (C-IL) becomes an important research direction. Hence, the problem of class incremental learning (C-IL) has been studied by the community for a while now (Kirkpatrick et al., 2017); yet, most of the previous work has focused on computer vision tasks (Cheng et al., 2019) with limited attention to NLP (Cao et al., 2020; Thorne and Vlachos, 2021).

A C-IL setup for regular releases of a model offers both challenges and opportunities. On the one hand, updating the previous model with new classes introduces a stability-plasticity problem (Mermillod et al., 2013), where the new model should both retain the knowledge about the old classes and learn the new classes on the same level of accuracy. On the other hand, re-using the old model to build the next release might help to reduce the reliance on old training data and speed up the training of the next release (Ash and Adams, 2020).

In this work, we compare contemporary solutions for incremental learning on a C-IL problem for the IC task following a production-inspired feature expansion cycle. We assume a number of consecutive model releases, where each one adds a number of new output classes and the corresponding training data. The training data for the old classes is either limited or not available at all in

[*] Work done at Amazon Alexa AI

Proceedings of the The First Workshop on Ever Evolving NLP (EvoNLP), pages 16 - 25
December 7, 2022 ©2022 Association for Computational Linguistics

line with the privacy requirements of a real-life setup, where there might be restrictions on storing or using older data.

We simulate this setup with the large intent classification OOS (Out-of-scope) dataset (Larson et al., 2019). Furthermore, we restrict our experiments to methods that do not increase the capacity of the final model with time. This is an important restriction in a real-world scenario where runtime constraints do not allow to make the model larger.

Our main contributions are:

1. To best of our knowledge, we are the first to explore different incremental learning methods for class-incremental learning in SLU in a data-scarce scenario.

2. We focus on the restriction of a production-like setup, where previous models might be available, but not the data and the runtime restriction prohibit making the model larger with time.

3. We present in-depth experiments on C-IL in two data-scenarios: without old data being available and with limited old, but unlabelled data being available. In the experiments, we compare the techniques that were previously proposed for fine-tuning and task-incremental learning and apply them repeatedly to extend the same model with new classes.

2 Related Work

2.1 Spoken language understanding

SLU has been mostly approached with deep learning methods (Mesnil et al., 2013) and specifically with large pre-trained models (Zhang and Wang, 2016; Chen et al., 2019; Louvan and Magnini, 2020). To improve the overall SLU performance, the community has investigated semi-supervised learning and paraphrasing to bootstrap new features and to overcome the class imbalance problem (Cho et al., 2019; Sokolov and Filimonov, 2020). The most research on SLU assumes that the number of classes is static, while in a real production SLU system, new classes are added on a regular basis. In contrast, in this work, we propose to focus on a C-IL scenario, where new classes are added to the system and the models needs to adapted in the absence of the previous training data.

2.2 Class-incremental learning

In a production environment, C-IL is a challenging problem since normally the new classes are only a small fraction of the classes in the new data.

Most approaches for incremental learning have been developed in the context of task-incremental learning and computer vision problems. In this paper, we study the importance of such methods on C-IL in NLP. There are several approaches that use regularization terms together with the classification loss in order to mitigate catastrophic forgetting. Few methods concentrate on the weights and estimate an importance metric for each parameter in the network (Kirkpatrick et al., 2017; Thorne and Vlachos, 2021) to decide what to update, while others focus on preventing the activation drift (Li and Hoiem, 2018).

Many previous works on continual learning have also focused on learning from a continuous stream of data (Biesialska et al., 2020) or on an incremental learning of new tasks (Kanwatchara et al., 2021) and languages (Castellucci et al., 2021). Payan et al. (2021) discuss a single-task continual learning setup and simulated a passive data extension scenario where new examples are coming in for all output classes on a public dataset. Similarly, Ash and Adams (2020) evaluate a batch-learning setup, where each model iteration is warm-started from the previous step and the whole training data is always available, while some new data is added across all output classes in each batch.

Finally, Wu et al. (2022) experiment on 5 different tasks to investigate the behaviour of fine-tuned large pre-trained models when the number of output classes grows with time. This setup is close to ours, as we also look at an expanding set of output intents in models. Uniquely, we focus on data-scarce scenarios, where old data might not be available anymore, which is motivated by privacy and production requirements of voice assistants.

3 Challenges

The fundamental obstacles to effective C-IL are conceptually simple, but in practice very challenging to overcome. These challenges originate from the sequential training of tasks and the requirement that at any moment the learner must be able to classify all classes from all previously learned tasks. Incremental learning methods must balance retaining knowledge from previous tasks while learning new knowledge for the current task. This problem is called the stability-plasticity dilemma (Mermillod et al., 2013). A naive approach to class incremental learning which focuses solely on learning the new task will suffer from catastrophic forgetting: a drastic drop in the performance on previous tasks. Preventing catastrophic forgetting leads to a second important problem of class incremental learning, i.e., the problem of intransigence: the resistance to learn new tasks. Class incremental learning methods need to balance between keeping knowledge about old classes and learning new classes at the same level of accuracy.

4 Method

We consider a C-IL scenario in which an existing NLP classification model is updated over time. We assume a number of consecutive model updates, and for each update, a certain number of new classes and corresponding training data become available, which need to be supported. Since, to the best of our knowledge, C-IL has not yet been explored for NLP classification tasks, this study includes a diverse set of techniques, which have shown promising results on other incremental learning tasks. In the following, we first describe our C-IL scenario in more detail. Subsequently, we discuss the considered basic classification model architecture and the C-IL strategies afterwards.

4.1 Class-incremental learning scenario

We assume that a task-specific classification model M_0 is available, which may already cover a comparatively large number of different output classes. Furthermore, we assume that we have access to an input stream of datasets D, each comprising labeled data for new classes: $D = [D_1, \ldots, D_n]$ with $D_i = \{(x_{i,j}, y_{i,j})\}_{j=1}^{|D_i|}$, where $x_{i,j_1}, \ldots, x_{i,j_n}$ is an utterance with n tokens, and $y_{i,j}$ is a sentence-level intent label. Each $D_i \in D$ comprises labeled data belonging to k_i new classes, i.e., classes which have not been observed during training of M_0 or in any of the previous datasets $D_1, \ldots, D_{i-1}$. For each dataset D_i, we perform a model update to integrate the new classes starting from the previous model M_{i-1}, yielding model M_i. More specifically, we assume that for each model update M_i

1. only the previous model M_{i-1} is available,

2. the dataset D_i comprising data belonging to k_i new classes is available, and

3. the datasets from previous iterations $D_1, \ldots, D_{i-1}$ are not available anymore.

In some of our experiments, we additionally assume that unlabeled data for classes from previous iterations are available.

In this class-incremental learning scenario, our goal is to add new classes over time, such that

1. a reasonable performance is attained on the data belonging to the new classes and

2. there is no catastrophic forgetting (performance degradation) on old classes.

4.2 Basic classification model architecture

Following the current state-of-the-art for production SLU models (Chen et al., 2019; Gaspers et al., 2021b,a; Weld et al., 2021), we consider classification model architectures that leverage large pretrained masked language models (MLM) for the models M_i. In particular, we assume that a model M_i consists of an MLM encoder and a task-specific classification head with softmax on top. We use cross-entropy loss for the classification task.

4.3 Class-incremental learning methods

We have selected five methods from different categories, including popular C-IL approaches based on weight regularization and on data regularization, which we summarize in the following.

Warm start (BERT) A naive C-IL strategy is simply to continue fine-tuning the previous model on new data. Recently, it has been shown that pretrained language models can effectively transfer task-agnostic knowledge to task-specific knowledge, and fine-tuning is a commonly used technique to mitigate model biases (Du et al., 2021). Therefore, "warm starting" the optimization rather than initializing randomly from scratch may be useful for quick adaptation to the new data and incorporating the new classes. However, on the downside, a direct pre-train-then-fine-tune approach is prone to catastrophic forgetting of previous knowledge (Ash and Adams, 2020).

Weight regularization-based approaches focus on preventing weight drift to consolidate previous knowledge when learning a new task. We include three methods that fall into this category: L2, Elastic Weight Consolidation (EWC) and RecAdam. As noted in the introduction, we only consider methods that do not increase model size with time, as this would be not restricted in a real-life runtime environment.

L2 When training on a new task, the importance of each parameter is used to penalize changes to them. Therefore, in addition to the classification loss (cross-entropy), we add an L2 regularised loss:

$$L(\theta^i) = L_{\text{cross}}(*) + \sum_{p}^{N} (\theta_p^{i-1} - \theta_p^i)^2, \quad (1)$$

where N = total number of parameters of $|\theta^{i-1}|$.

EWC Kirkpatrick et al. (2017) proposed *Elastic Weight Consolidation* (EWC) that is a weight regularization method that penalizes parameter updates according to the model's sensitivity. The model sensitivity is calculated as a diagonal approximation of the Fisher Information Matrix F_i, which captures the importance of the model at the minimum after each task is learned, while ignoring the influence of those parameters along the learning trajectory in weight space. The modified loss with EWC is defined as:

$$L(\theta^i) = L_{\text{cross}}(*) + \sum_{p}^{N} \frac{\lambda}{2} F_p(\theta_p^{i-1} - \theta_p^i)^2 \quad (2)$$

where N = total number of parameters of $|\theta^{i-1}|$.

RecAdam. Recently, Chen et al. (2020) proposed RecAdam to address the problem of sequential transferring regime of deep pre-trained LMs. They assume that the pre-training data is not available during fine-tuning on a new task. They propose an optimizer that consists of two modules: Pre-training Simulation and Objective Shifting, where the former allows the model to learn source tasks without pre-training data, and the latter allows the model to focus on target tasks. Recadam was motivated by EWC and it keeps a copy of the pretrained parameters and accesses them at each training step. Recadam introduces a quadratic penalty between pretrained and fine-tuned weights in the optimization objective to prevent deviating from the pre-trained model weights. In our class incremental learning setting, we also keep the model's parameters trained on previous classes and access them for training on new class data.

Knowledge distillation. Knowledge distillation (KD) was initially proposed by Hinton et al. (2015) to encourage the outputs of one model to approximate the outputs of another, and hence it can be applied to prevent activation drift. In this study, we adopted the Teacher-Student framework for KD. In our case, at C-IL stage i, the teacher is the model M_{i-1} which was already trained on the previous datasets. The student model is a clone of the teacher, which is fine-tuned using a combined loss function:

$$L = (1 - \lambda)L_{\text{cross}} + \lambda L_{KD}, \quad (3)$$

where L_{cross} is the task-specific cross-entropy loss, which is computed on the new dataset D_i. The knowledge distillation loss L_{KD} is computed as the cross-entropy between the output probability distributions provided by the student and teacher models. λ is a hyper-parameter balancing the two losses. We set the hyper-parameter λ to $\frac{k_{old}}{k_{old}+k_{new}}$ where k is the number of classes.

Note in all of the above setups we initialize (warm-start) the next model M^i with the previous M^{i-1} model.

5 Experimental set up

In our experiments, we study two C-IL scenarios: without any old data available and assuming that a small amount of unlabeled data for old classes can be accessed. In the following, we first discuss both scenarios in more detail. Subsequently, we describe the dataset and class-incremental learning simulation, and finally the experimental settings.

5.1 Class-incremental learning scenarios

In our experiments, we study the following two class-incremental learning scenarios:

1. **Core C-IL scenario with no previous data.** This scenario can be referred to as the "true" class-incremental learning scenario described in section 4.1 and this is the most extreme scenario for incremental learning. We assume that at C-IL stage *i* we only have access to the previous model M_{i-1} and the new dataset D_i covering new classes. However, **no data** corresponding to previous classes is available. We study this scenario because storing data for long is often impossible and training a model from scratch is expensive in real-world scenarios. Therefore, we assume that we only have a previously trained model available but no old exemplars (i.e., no data corresponding to old classes) in this setting.

	Limited unlabeled data		Core C-IL no previous data		
IS	Train	TC	Train	TC	Dev/Test
0	5000	1-50	5000	1-50	1000/1500
1	1250	1-70	1000	51-70	1400/2100
2	1350	1-90	1000	71-90	1800/2700
3	1450	1-110	1000	91-110	2200/3300
4	1550	1-130	1000	111-130	2600/3900
5	1650	1-150	1000	131-150	3000/4500

Table 1: Data statistics for the IL setup on the OOS datase. **IS**: Incremental stage, **Train**: available training data at each stage, **TC**: Included training classes.

2. **Limited unlabeled data availability C-IL scenario**. In this scenario, we assume that a limited amount of **unlabeled** data for older classes is available. While we are aiming for a technique that succeeds in scenario 1, this is a very challenging problem to solve. On the other hand, in real-world settings, some unlabeled data of previous classes sometimes can be collected again or stored for a short period. Thus, scenario 2 is also reasonable and included for comparison regarding what performance can be reached when a small amount of unlabeled data of previous classes is available vs. unavailable. In this scenario, we additionally leverage semi-supervised learning and we use the previous model M_{i-1} to label the unlabeled data at the incremental stage i. Note that unlabeled data are much less expensive than labeled data as no annotators are needed, and it is preferable w.r.t. privacy concerns, as no human needs to look into the utterances to annotate them.

In both cases, we assume that an initial model M_0 is trained first, covering 50 intent classes. Subsequently, five incremental learning stages are conducted, and in each stage 20 new classes are added.

5.2 Data

We evaluate our models using the out-of-scope (OOS) dataset (Larson et al., 2019) for intent classification. The OOS dataset comprises English user queries which were annotated with intents. It contains 150 intent classes, and our goal is that model's learn these 150 classes incrementally.

For class-incremental learning experiments, we first randomly selected 50 classes and used all corresponding training and development data for training the initial model M_0. Next, we randomly split the remaining classes into 5 groups, each comprising 20 classes, and we created datasets by collecting the data for the groups of classes. This process resulted in datasets covering 5 incremental stages (IS), which we split to create training, development and test sets for each incremental stage.

To simulate the second C-IL scenario with limited unlabeled data amounts for old classes, we set 5% of data aside per class and dropped labels. Next, we use the previously trained model (M_{i-1}) to annotate the unlabeled data for the next incremental stage and add the annotated data to the new labeled training data.

The data splits and statistics are reported in Table 1. The number of exemplars per class in each incremental phase is uniform.

5.3 Hyperparameter details and metrics

We use the BERT-large-uncased model from the Huggingface Transformers package. The BERT architecture type is widely used in practical applications[1] and we limit our experiments to this common architecture type and instead choose to evaluate multiple scenarios and C-IL methods (see Section 5). We train five random initializations of each model, reporting the mean accuracy for all of the experiments. This results in over 180 experimental runs for the two setups, the five tested methods and the oracle. For fine-tuning, the learning rate and regularization strength are selected through 5-fold cross-validation on the BERT warm start train data, selecting the model with the highest training accuracy. We choose the regularization strength λ from $\{10^6, 2{*}10^6, 10^7, 2{*}10^7\}$ and three learning rates in $\{2 * 10^6, 4 * 10^6, 6 * 10^6\}$. We also use the following hyperparameters: (a) Embedding dimension: 768, (b) Optimizer: AdamW, and (c) Gradient Norm: 10.0. Our main evaluation metric at each incremental step is the standard multi-class accuracy. We report overall accuracy results, as well as the break down for old and new classes.

6 Experimental Results

Recall that the core challenge with class incremental learning methods is to balance retaining knowledge from old exemplars while learning new knowledge for the new exemplars. In our experiments, we investigate how the different incremental learning methods perform on both preventing *catastrophic forgetting* and *intransigence* i.e., resistance to learn

[1]C.f. the number of downloads in the last months for BERT models `https://huggingface.co/models?sort=downloads&search=bert`

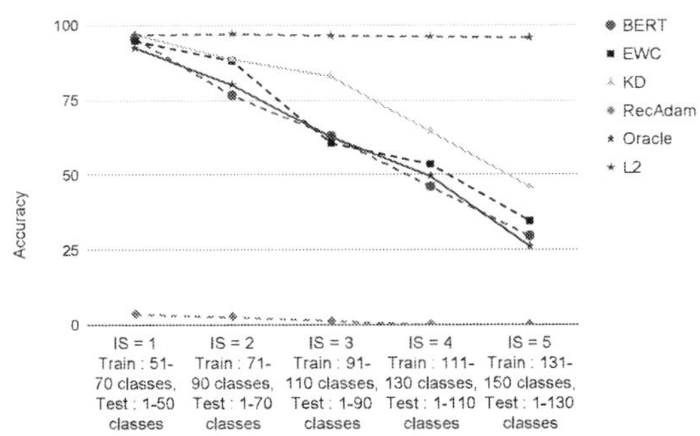

Figure 1: Average accuracy of the C-IL methods on all seen classes so far until the previous incremental phase for the core C-IL scenario.

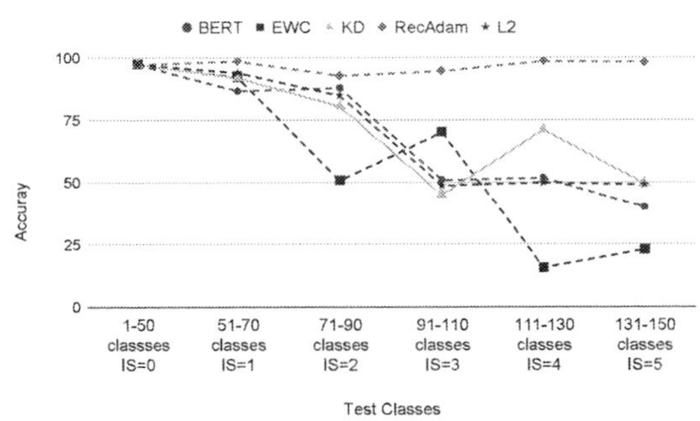

Figure 2: Accuracy of the C-IL methods methods on new class labels at different IL stages for the core C-IL scenario.

about new exemplars. Where appropriate, we also include performance of an "oracle"; contrasting with the C-IL techniques, the oracle has access to all of the previously available labeled datasets. It should be seen as an upper bound, indicating what performance would be possible if older labeled data could be kept for model training.

6.1 Core C-IL scenario

Forgetting over time We first study the performance of the C-IL methods in addressing the catastrophic forgetting problem. Figure 1 compares the different C-IL methods on old class labels at different incremental learning stages. Firstly, we observe that the KD method performs consistently better than other C-IL methods in the trend of accuracy at different incremental learning stages. Next, we find that RecAdam suffers the most significant performance drop. Interestingly, the performance of EWC until incremental stage (IS) 3 is comparable to BERT WARM-START and L2. However, as the number of incremental stages increases, the performance of BERT WARM-START and L2 comparatively drops more.

We also report the upper bound results denoted as *Oracle* where models are trained with all training data of the classes learned so far. The gap in performance of KD and EWC appears unbridgeable after IS 2. This suggests that (1) only constraining old parameters does not suffice to prevent forgetting and (2) there is a positive effect of the distribution information of previous features in C-IL.

Performance on new exemplars To analyze the effectiveness of different C-IL models more concretely, we explore how they affect the new class label's accuracy. Figure 2 shows the performance of different methods on newer class labels at different incremental phases. We find that RecAdam performs better on the new class labels. The RecAdam optimizer was designed to improve the model's performance on the fine-tuning task by not deviating too much from the pretrained model parameters. This could be an intuitive reason for RecAdam's strong performance on newer class labels. This also aligns with the poor performance of RecAdam on the older exemplars (see Figure 1).

We observe that BERT WARM-START performs better than KD on new class labels at the earlier incremental stages. However, when the number of stages increases, the KD method outperforms BERT WARM-START and EWC in learning about the new class labels and remembering previous labels (see Figure 1). This indicates that the performance of the KD method is better in reducing the forgetting problem and performs better on newer class labels when we increase the number of incremental stages.

Analysis Tables 2a-2e present the performance with respect to *average Accuracy* and *Forgetting Rates* of each method at different incremental stages. The last column (red cells) of each table represents the *average accuracy*:

$$\overline{A} = \frac{1}{N+1}\sum_{i=0}^{N} A_i, \qquad (4)$$

where A_i is accuracy on the test dataset D_i^{test} comprising data belonging to the k_i batch of classes. For example, the $\overline{A}$ column at M_1, M_2,.., M_5 represents the performance on classes 1-70, 1-90, .., 1-150 respectively. The diagonal cells represent the performance of each method on new class labels (this is also the data visualized in Figure 2). In this case, *IS*=1, *IS*=2,.., *IS*=5 means the performance on classes $51-70$, $71-90$, .., $131-150$ respectively.

The lower triangle (**blue cells**) of each table represents *Forgetting Rates* (lower is better) : $F = A_{i,i} - A_{i,j}$, where $j < i$. Similar to (Liu et al., 2020), we define a forgetting rate, denoted as F, by calculating the difference between the accuracy of the old model (M_k) and the new model (M_{k+i}) on the same test data. For example, in Table 2a, the M_1 model at *IS*=0 (i.e., performance on 1-50 classes) forgets 1.81 accuracy points with respect to the model M_0.

The bold numbers represent the best performing model at different incremental stages. There are two main observations: (1) For class incremental learning, we hypothesize that the model is prone to suffer from more severe forgetting as the incremental stage increases. We find that although there was some big drop after training on the 3rd incremental stage, KD forgetting rate is low. Interestingly, the forgetting rate for EWC is relatively low. We find that with the EWC method the results at some incremental phases have negative forgetting rates suggesting that a new model (such as M_3, M_4, M_5) performs better than the corresponding previous model for some old classes. One intuitive reason could be that the performance on the new labels for EWC is comparatively poor compared to BERT WARM-START and the KD method. KD maintains stable performance as the number of incremental stages increases. Especially after training on the 4th and 5th stage, the forgetting increment was relatively small, which demonstrated the robustness of KD. (2) After each individual phase, the learned model M_i is evaluated on the test data $D^{test}_{0:i}$, where $0:i$ denotes all seen classes so far. We observe that initially all methods except RECADAM work well but as the incremental phase increases to 5th, the KD method gains $+14.2$ pp.

	Forgetting Rate						
	IS=0	**IS=1**	**IS=2**	**IS=3**	**IS=4**	**IS=5**	$\overline{A}$
M_0	97.4						
M_1	**1.81**	86.66					92.3
M_2	9.55	38.36	87.83				80.6
M_3	22.15	35.66	24.83	51			59.3
M_4	30.03	63.66	45.33	31.5	51.8		49.0
M_5	**38.03**	71.5	71.67	46	43.97	40.0	29.1

(a) BERT Warm Start

	Forgetting Rate						
	IS=0	**IS=1**	**IS=2**	**IS=3**	**IS=4**	**IS=5**	$\overline{A}$
M_0	97.4						
M_1	2.74	92.16					93.57
M_2	**3.81**	18.16	50.83				81.2
M_3	21.55	65.33	-5.17	70.16			56.08
M_4	29.43	64.16	-4.33	**29.16**	15.66		47.41
M_5	39.7	77.5	26.83	56.66	-12.67	23.0	29.6

(b) EWC

	Forgetting Rate						
	IS=0	**IS=1**	**IS=2**	**IS=3**	**IS=4**	**IS=5**	$\overline{A}$
M_0	97.4						
M_1	2.6	92					**94.6**
M_2	6.88	**8**	80.5				**82.6**
M_3	**11,75**	**11.5**	**1.84**	45			**72.66**
M_4	**20.55**	**18**	**11.65**	23.4	71.11		**55.17**
M_5	40.7	**44.17**	**39.39**	**31.34**	**16.45**	49.5	**43.8**

(c) KD

	Forgetting Rate						
	IS=0	**IS=1**	**IS=2**	**IS=3**	**IS=4**	**IS=5**	$\overline{A}$
M_0	97.4						
M_1	5	94					92.8
M_2	10.14	31.84	84.3				81.18
M_3	19.87	54	35.8	48.66			60.1
M_4	24.4	64	38	34.5	49.83		49.66
M_5	48.8	81	67.3	45.86	34.08	49	29.22

(d) L2

	Forgetting Rate						
	IS=0	**IS=1**	**IS=2**	**IS=3**	**IS=4**	**IS=5**	$\overline{A}$
M_0	97.2						
M_1	93.5	**98.5**					30.66
M_2	93.47	98.5	**92.8**				22.70
M_3	95	98.5	92.8	**94.66**			18.30
M_4	97.4	98.5	92.8	94.66	**98.66**		15.17
M_5	97.4	98.5	92.8	94.66	98.66	**98.16**	13.08

(e) RecAdam

Table 2: Performance of each method with respect to average accuracy (last column) and forgetting rates (lower triangle) at different IS. For average accuracy higher is better, for forgetting rates lower is better.

6.2 Limited unlabeled data available

Motivated by our findings in the supervised setting, in this scenario, we assume that we have a small amount of unlabelled data corresponding to previous class labels available. We use the previously trained model to automatically annotate the unlabelled data and add this data into the training set for training the model for the next phase.

Figure 3 presents the results of the different C-IL methods on class labels seen so far until the previous incremental learning stages. Firstly, we observe that the performance of all C-IL methods benefits from the extra data. Interestingly, the performance of the EWC method is much more stable than without any previously labelled data. Moreover, the KD method still performs relatively bet-

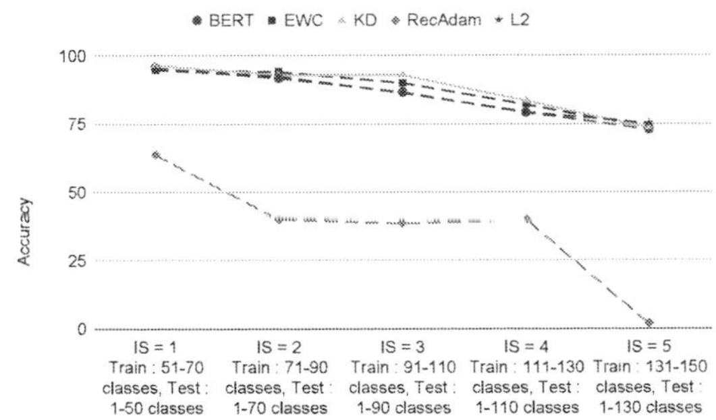

Figure 3: Average accuracy in the setting where limited unlabeled data is available for the C-IL methods on all seen classes so far until the previous incremental phase.

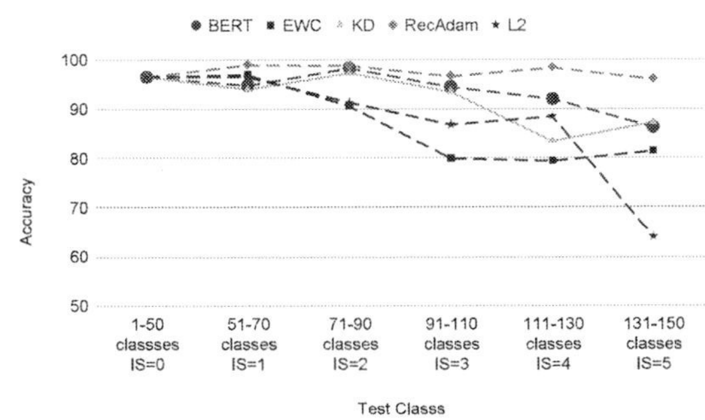

Figure 4: Accuracy in the setting where limited unlabeled data is available for the C-IL methods on new class labels at different incremental learning stages.

ter than other methods in preventing the forgetting problem. Figure 4 depicts the performance on the newer class labels at each incremental phase. BERT WARM-START works better than the KD and EWC methods, indicating that extra noisy data helps BERT WARM-START more. Similar to Figure 2 we observe that RECADAM performs better on newer class labels, indicating that it is over-fitted to newer exemplars.

The average accuracy results are shown in Table 3. The EWC and KD methods perform best by a large margin. EWC shows a small gain for the first couple of incremental phases compared with KD and L2. However, the gain increases as more incremental phases are conducted. Regarding the final incremental classifier on all classes, the KD method outperforms EWC, L2 and BERT WARM-START by 0.8%, 2% and 2.44% respectively.

7 Conclusion

In this paper, we explored class-incremental learning for the intent classification task. In particular, we compared several methods, i.e., BERT warm start, L2, Elastic Weight Consolidation, RecAdam and Knowledge Distillation. We compared performance within two class-incremental learning scenarios: one where only the previous model was assumed to be available, but no data corresponding to old classes, and one in which limited unlabeled data for old classes was assumed to be available.

We are the first to benchmark these methods in the challenging incremental learning setup for intent classification motivated by real-life restrictions where no old data might be available. We presented extensive experiments on the out-of-scope dataset for intent classification. Among the investigated continual learning methods, Knowledge Distillation worked best for our class-incremental learning tasks, and adding limited unlabeled data helped the model in both adaptability and stability. We plan to add token-level slot prediction task to our setup in the future and include further MLM models beyond just the BERT architecture.

Test classes	70	90	110	130	150
Method	M_1	M_2	M_3	M_4	M_5
BERT Warm-start	95.52	91.5	86.81	80.2	73.06
EWC	95.4	93.4	88.18	81.7	74.7
KD	95.7	91.7	89.18	82.5	75.5
RecAdam	73.8	53.22	49.18	48.89	14.2
L2	95.38	92.25	86.5	80.8	73.5

Table 3: *Average Accuracy* of different C-IL methods in the setting where limited unlabeled data is available.

8 Ethical considerations

The experiments presented in this paper are performed with publicly available models and methods on a public dataset and can be verified independently. Our experimental setup is motivated by a real-life problem of regular SLU model releases, where it is critical to maintain the performance on old classes and not to introduce new errors into the existing model so that no user is negatively affected by the changes. The incremental learning techniques discussed here have a potential to improve user privacy, as they do not rely on storing the old data. Training only on the data incremental has also a significant impact on model training times and resource usage and, as a consequences, improves the environmental impact of a model release pipeline.

References

Jordan Ash and Ryan P Adams. 2020. On warm-starting neural network training. *Advances in Neural Information Processing Systems*, 33:3884–3894.

Magdalena Biesialska, Katarzyna Biesialska, and Marta R. Costa-jussà. 2020. Continual lifelong learning in natural language processing: A survey. In *Proceedings of the 28th International Conference on Computational Linguistics*, pages 6523–6541, Barcelona, Spain (Online). International Committee on Computational Linguistics.

Pengfei Cao, Yubo Chen, Jun Zhao, and Taifeng Wang. 2020. Incremental event detection via knowledge consolidation networks. In *Proceedings of the 2020 Conference on Empirical Methods in Natural Language Processing (EMNLP)*, pages 707–717, Online. Association for Computational Linguistics.

Giuseppe Castellucci, Simone Filice, Danilo Croce, and Roberto Basili. 2021. Learning to solve NLP tasks in an incremental number of languages. In *Proceedings of the 59th Annual Meeting of the Association for Computational Linguistics and the 11th International Joint Conference on Natural Language Processing (Volume 2: Short Papers)*, pages 837–847, Online. Association for Computational Linguistics.

Qian Chen, Zhu Zhuo, and Wen Wang. 2019. BERT for Joint Intent Classification and Slot Filling. *arXiv preprint arXiv:1902.10909*.

Sanyuan Chen, Yutai Hou, Yiming Cui, Wanxiang Che, Ting Liu, and Xiangzhan Yu. 2020. Recall and learn: Fine-tuning deep pretrained language models with less forgetting. In *Proceedings of the 2020 Conference on Empirical Methods in Natural Language Processing (EMNLP)*, pages 7870–7881, Online. Association for Computational Linguistics.

Hao Cheng, Dongze Lian, Bowen Deng, Shenghua Gao, Tao Tan, and Yanlin Geng. 2019. Local to global learning: Gradually adding classes for training deep neural networks. In *Proceedings of the IEEE/CVF Conference on Computer Vision and Pattern Recognition*, pages 4748–4756.

Eunah Cho, He Xie, and William M Campbell. 2019. Paraphrase generation for semi-supervised learning in nlu. In *Proceedings of the Workshop on Methods for Optimizing and Evaluating Neural Language Generation*, pages 45–54.

Tom Diethe, Tom Borchert, Eno Thereska, Borja Balle, and Neil D Lawrence. 2018. Continual learning in practice. In *Proceedings of the NeurIPS 2018 workshop on Continual Learning*.

Li Du, Xiao Ding, Ting Liu, and Bing Qin. 2021. Learning event graph knowledge for abductive reasoning. In *Proceedings of the 59th Annual Meeting of the Association for Computational Linguistics and the 11th International Joint Conference on Natural Language Processing (Volume 1: Long Papers)*, pages 5181–5190, Online. Association for Computational Linguistics.

Judith Gaspers, Quynh Do, Tobias Röding, and Melanie Bradford. 2021a. The impact of domain-specific representations on BERT-based multi-domain spoken language understanding. In *Proceedings of the Second Workshop on Domain Adaptation for NLP*, pages 28–32, Kyiv, Ukraine. Association for Computational Linguistics.

Judith Gaspers, Quynh Do, Daniil Sorokin, and Patrick Lehnen. 2021b. The Impact of Intent Distribution Mismatch on Semi-Supervised Spoken Language Understanding. In *Proc. Interspeech 2021*, pages 4708–4712.

Geoffrey Hinton, Oriol Vinyals, and Jeffrey Dean. 2015. Distilling the knowledge in a neural network. In *NIPS Deep Learning and Representation Learning Workshop*.

Kasidis Kanwatchara, Thanapapas Horsuwan, Piyawat Lertvittayakumjorn, Boonserm Kijsirikul, and Peerapon Vateekul. 2021. Rational LAMOL: A rationale-based lifelong learning framework. In *Proceedings of the 59th Annual Meeting of the Association for Computational Linguistics and the 11th International Joint Conference on Natural Language Processing (Volume 1: Long Papers)*, pages 2942–2953, Online. Association for Computational Linguistics.

James Kirkpatrick, Razvan Pascanu, Neil C. Rabinowitz, Joel Veness, Guillaume Desjardins, Andrei A. Rusu, Kieran Milan, John Quan, Tiago Ramalho, Agnieszka Grabska-Barwinska, Demis Hassabis, Claudia Clopath, Dharshan Kumaran, and Raia Hadsell. 2017. Overcoming catastrophic forgetting in neural networks. *Proceedings of the National Academy of Sciences*, 114:3521 – 3526.

Stefan Larson, Anish Mahendran, Joseph J. Peper, Christopher Clarke, Andrew Lee, Parker Hill, Jonathan K. Kummerfeld, Kevin Leach, Michael A. Laurenzano, Lingjia Tang, and Jason Mars. 2019. An evaluation dataset for intent classification and out-of-scope prediction. In *Proceedings of the 2019 Conference on Empirical Methods in Natural Language Processing and the 9th International Joint Conference on Natural Language Processing (EMNLP-IJCNLP)*, pages 1311–1316, Hong Kong, China. Association for Computational Linguistics.

Zhizhong Li and Derek Hoiem. 2018. Learning without forgetting. *IEEE Transactions on Pattern Analysis and Machine Intelligence*, 40:2935–2947.

Yaoyao Liu, Anan Liu, Yuting Su, Bernt Schiele, and Qianru Sun. 2020. Mnemonics training: Multi-class incremental learning without forgetting. *2020 IEEE/CVF Conference on Computer Vision and Pattern Recognition (CVPR)*, pages 12242–12251.

Samuel Louvan and Bernardo Magnini. 2020. Recent neural methods on slot filling and intent classification for task-oriented dialogue systems: A survey. In *Proceedings of the 28th International Conference on Computational Linguistics*, pages 480–496, Barcelona, Spain (Online). International Committee on Computational Linguistics.

Martial Mermillod, Aurélia Bugaiska, and Patrick BONIN. 2013. The stability-plasticity dilemma: investigating the continuum from catastrophic forgetting to age-limited learning effects. *Frontiers in Psychology*, 4.

Grégoire Mesnil, Xiaodong He, Li Deng, and Yoshua Bengio. 2013. Investigation of Recurrent-Neural-Network Architectures and Learning Methods for Spoken Language Understanding. In *Interspeech*, pages 3771–3775, Lyon, France.

Justin Payan, Yuval Merhav, He Xie, Satyapriya Krishna, Anil Ramakrishna, Mukund Sridhar, and Rahul Gupta. 2021. Towards realistic single-task continuous learning research for NER. In *Findings of the Association for Computational Linguistics: EMNLP 2021*, pages 3773–3783, Punta Cana, Dominican Republic. Association for Computational Linguistics.

Alex Sokolov and Denis Filimonov. 2020. Neural machine translation for paraphrase generation. *arXiv preprint arXiv:2006.14223*.

James Thorne and Andreas Vlachos. 2021. Elastic weight consolidation for better bias inoculation. In *Proceedings of the 16th Conference of the European Chapter of the Association for Computational Linguistics: Main Volume*, pages 957–964, Online. Association for Computational Linguistics.

H. Weld, X. Huang, S. Long, J. Poon, and S. C. Han. 2021. A survey of joint intent detection and slot-filling models in natural language understanding.

Tongtong Wu, Massimo Caccia, Zhuang Li, Yuan-Fang Li, Guilin Qi, and Gholamreza Haffari. 2022. Pretrained language model in continual learning: A comparative study. In *International Conference on Learning Representations*.

Xiaodong Zhang and Houfeng Wang. 2016. A Joint Model of Intent Determination and Slot Filling for Spoken Language Understanding. In *Proceedings of the Twenty-Fifth IJCAI*, page 2993–2999, New York, NY, USA.

CC-Top: Constrained Clustering for Dynamic Topic Discovery

Jann Goschenhofer[1,2♠] **Pranav Ragupathy**[1♣] **Christian Heumann**[1♠] **Bernd Bischl**[1,2,3♠]
Matthias Aßenmacher[1♠]
[1] Department of Statistics, LMU, Munich, Germany
[2] Fraunhofer IIS, Erlangen, Germany
[3] Munich Center for Machine Learning (MCML), LMU, Munich, Germany
♠{jann.goschenhofer,chris,bernd.bischl,matthias}@stat.uni-muenchen.de
♣p.ragupathy@campus.lmu.de

Abstract

Research on multi-class text classification of short texts mainly focuses on supervised (transfer) learning approaches, requiring a finite set of pre-defined classes which is constant over time. This work explores deep constrained clustering (CC) as an alternative to supervised learning approaches in a setting with a dynamically changing number of classes, a task we introduce as *dynamic topic discovery* (DTD). We do so by using pairwise similarity constraints instead of instance-level class labels which allow for a flexible number of classes while exhibiting a competitive performance compared to supervised approaches. First, we substantiate this through a series of experiments and show that CC algorithms exhibit a predictive performance similar to state-of-the-art supervised learning algorithms while requiring less annotation effort. Second, we demonstrate the overclustering capabilities of deep CC for detecting topics in short text data sets in the absence of the ground truth class cardinality during model training. Third, we showcase how these capabilities can be leveraged for the DTD setting as a step towards dynamic learning over time. Finally, we release our codebase to nurture further research in this area.

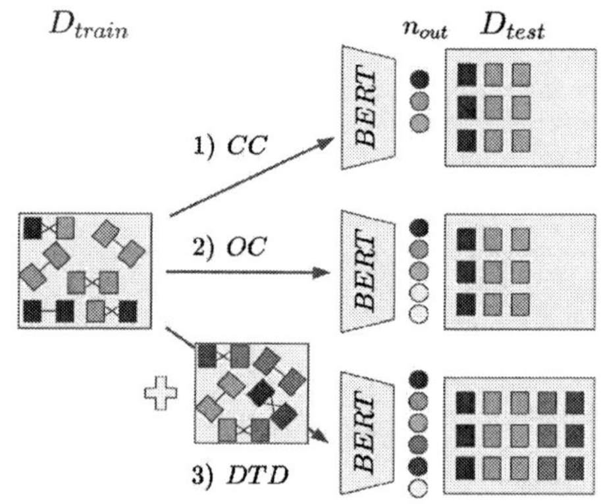

Figure 1: Illustration of CC-Top and the training paradigms 1) constrained clustering (CC), 2) overclustering (OC) and 3) dynamic topic discovery (DTD). Crosses and lines represent Cannot- and Must-Link pairwise relations, respectively.

1 Introduction

There has been substantial research on methods for the classification of short user-generated texts such as customer reviews, search queries, tweets, or articles (Mohammad et al., 2016; Sun et al., 2019; Barbieri et al., 2020). Often, despite being handled differently in supervised frameworks, one does not know *a-priori* what these classes are, how many there are at time point t, or how many there will be at a future time point $t+1$. In existing benchmark data sets from the natural language processing (NLP) research community (e.g. Lang, 1995; Lehmann et al., 2015), this potential issue is largely ignored, since only one training set is provided alongside one test set. Performance can thus only be measured in a static fashion, i.e. for one fixed time point. While this problem of an unknown number of classes is often tackled using unsupervised learning techniques (Deerwester et al., 1990; Blei et al., 2003), these algorithms come with an array of limitations and are not able to (automatically) adapt to a changing number of classes. We formally introduce this novel problem setting with dynamically changing topics as DTD and explore the potential of deep constrained clustering (CC; Hsu et al., 2019) algorithms coupled with pre-trained language models (BERT; Devlin et al., 2019) for text classification in this setting.

Various approaches have been developed to combine CC (Wagstaff and Cardie, 2000) with neural networks, mainly for image datasets (Hsu and Kira, 2015; Hsu et al., 2019). In addition to strong predictive clustering performance, these methods are able to recover the number of distinct clusters in the data without access to instance-level class labels during training. Hence, they can be used for category detection, a capability that we leverage for the detection of dynamically changing topics.

Proceedings of the The First Workshop on Ever Evolving NLP (EvoNLP), pages 26 - 34
December 7, 2022 ©2022 Association for Computational Linguistics

Moreover, they address and alleviate the problem of label annotation: Human annotators only need to annotate pairs of samples indicating whether they belong to a similar topic or not instead of annotating one distinct class label per sample. We argue that for short texts this is easier and more efficient than annotating individual samples.

We propose the use of **C**onstrained **C**lustering for **Top**ic classification (CC-Top, cf. Fig. 1): We 1) leverage pairwise constraint annotations for topic classification of short texts in a weakly supervised manner, we 2) demonstrate its topic discovery capabilities and 3) introduce a new problem setting with dynamically changing topics. In a series of experiments, we substantiate these findings and publish our codebase[1] to nurture further research on constrained clustering in the NLP community.

2 Related Work

With the advent of supervised fine-tuning of pretrained models, text clustering performance further increased (Huang et al., 2020; Schopf et al., 2021). One main limitation of these models is their dependence on a given amount of clusters as input for model training, which limits their use for the detection of clusters, i.e., topics/classes. Unsupervised topic modeling algorithms (e.g. Blei et al., 2003; Grootendorst, 2022) are no real alternative here, since we focus on topic *classification* and not on topic *modeling*. Note, that we make a clear distinction between these two approaches here: Topic modeling aims at uncovering latent structures in the data and puts a large emphasis on explaining and interpreting the detected clusters. Further, as opposed to *Topic classification*, it does not assume the cluster assignment to be mutually exclusive, i.e. a document is regarded as a (potential) mixture of multiple topics. Since this is in sharp contrast to the setting we are investigating, we do not consider such approaches as potential unsupervised baselines.

In turn, CC allows this detection of the number of clusters using binary pairwise constraint annotations. The introduction of pairwise constraints for clustering (Wagstaff and Cardie, 2000) led to the adaptation of existing clustering methods towards the use of constraints (Basu et al., 2004) (see Gançarski et al. (2020) for an overview). With the proposal of the KCL loss based on the Kullback-Leibler divergence, Hsu and Kira (2016) introduced CC to deep learning settings. They further showed its applicability to transfer learning (Hsu et al., 2018), introduced the MCL as an alternative loss (Hsu et al., 2019), and showed its applicability for cluster detection, i.e., overclustering. We use these two pairwise loss functions.

[1] https://github.com/rpranav22/cc-top

3 Materials and Methods

3.1 Method

We consider a dataset $\mathcal{D}$ that contains n_c constraint pairs of the form $x_{ij} = (x_i, x_j, c_{ij}) \in \mathcal{D}^c$, where x_i, x_j are two input samples and $c_{ij} \in \{0, 1\}$ is the associated binary constraint describing whether the samples are in the same ($c_{ij} = 1$, *Must-Link*) or different clusters ($c_{ij} = 0$, *Cannot-Link*). We refer to true class labels as $y_i \in \mathcal{Y}$, where $K = |\mathcal{Y}|$ describes the number of true underlying classes K in the data set. When K is not known, the model's number of output neurons n_{out} may differ from K. We train a deep CC model f with its final head consisting of a softmax layer i.e., the model predicts a probability distribution over cluster assignments $\hat{y}_i = f(x_i)$, where $\hat{y}_{il}$ denotes the predicted probability of x_i belonging to cluster $l \in 1, ..., n_{out}$.

We follow Hsu and Kira (2016); Hsu et al. (2019) for the training of the CC model: the model predictions $\hat{y}_i, \hat{y}_j$ for text samples x_i, x_j are fed into a pairwise loss function with their associated constraint c_{ij}. There exists a variety of loss functions that can deal with pairwise constraints (Zhang et al., 2021b), with the KCL (Hsu and Kira, 2016) and the MCL (Hsu et al., 2019) being the most prominent ones. The KCL is a pairwise loss function based on the Kullback-Leibler divergence between the pairwise model assignments $\hat{y}_i, \hat{y}_j$. Similarly, the MCL loss is aligned on the binary cross entropy loss and reportedly enables smoother model training. Following prior work (Lin et al., 2020; Zhang et al., 2021a), we use BERT (Devlin et al., 2019) as a language model backbone for f.[2] Note that throughout our experiments we randomly subsample a training dataset of $20,000$ pairwise constraints from the original fully labeled dataset.

Next to the application in settings where the true number of clusters K is known a-priori, CC models can also be used when this information is absent during model training. This is also referred to as overclustering (OC) where the model can

[2] Note that any (pre-trained) architecture can be used as a backbone in conjunction with these loss functions. All configurations can be found in Table 5 in Appendix A.

assign more clusters than present in the data, i.e. $n_{out} > K$. This capability to learn the number of clusters in the data from constraint annotations differentiates CC from clustering methods such as k-means, where K needs to be provided as a hyper-parameter to the model, or supervised approaches.

3.2 Baselines

As a lower, unsupervised baseline, we use BERT embeddings combined with K-MEANS++ (Arthur and Vassilvitskii, 2006). For the fully supervised upper bound trained via instance-level class labels, we finetune the BERT-BASE-UNCASED architecture from huggingface (Wolf et al., 2020), following the standard pretrain-finetune paradigm. Both baselines are trained on the entire training dataset.

3.3 Dynamic Topic Discovery (DTD)

We now consider the scenario, where the set of classes is not fixed and known *a-priori* at time point t but is dynamically changing over time ($t+1, t+2, \ldots$): First, at t, we have pairwise annotations for samples that belong to K_t distinct classes. Second, we train a CC model f_t to assign any new data point to one of the discovered clusters. Third, at $t+1$, we obtain new samples that could either belong to one of the initial K_t classes or to new, unseen classes and the model fails to classify the new samples accurately.

If our model was fully supervised (i.e., trained on instance-level class labels), we would have to reconsider the entire labeling scheme (i.e., produce the new classes and revisit all existing labeled samples from t) and re-train the entire model. However, in the case of CC, we can continue annotating the data using pairwise constraints and continue to train the existing model (i.e., let the model determine (i) if there are new classes and (ii) how many of them). We construct the following scenario to investigate the model's capability to adapt to a changing number of classes over time: First, we fix the architectural setup to CC-KCL on DBpedia and use $n_{out} = 30$ to provide the model with enough over-clustering flexibility. Second, for $t = 1$, we take a subset of the training set, consisting of samples from 10 classes only, and sample $n_c = 20,000$ constraints from this subset, resulting in $38,056$ samples from 10 classes for training ($D_{train,t=1}$). Third, for $t = 2$, we select $18,000$ samples from the remainder of the training set ($D_{train,t=2}$) controlling for the ratio of the classes that the samples belong to $x\%$ from the 'old' 10 classes at $t = 1$ and $(100 - x)\%$ from the 'new' 4 classes at $t = 2$, which were withheld from $D_{train,t=1}$. The DBpedia test set is also split into two distinct parts: $D_{test,1}$ contains only samples from the 10 'old' classes, and $D_{test,2}$ contains only samples from the 4 'new' ones. During the DTD experiments, we denote the entire test set as $D_{test,combined}$.

3.4 Datasets

We run experiments on three English datasets of short texts with associated instance-level class labels. An overview of the analyzed data sets AG News (Zhang et al., 2015), TREC coarse (Li and Roth, 2002), and DBpedia (Lehmann et al., 2015) is provided in Table 1. We did not perform any further special preprocessing. We used only DBPedia for further experiments with respect to DTD, since the number of classes in the other two data sets was too small to construct a meaningful DTD scenario.

Name	K	$\#Train$	$\#Val$	$\#Test$	Avg. Length
AG News	4	120,000	8,000	7,600	40
TREC coarse	6	4,952	500	500	10
DBpedia	14	560,000	35,000	35,000	50

Table 1: Overview of the data sets used for evaluation.

3.5 Performance Metrics

Following prior work (Hsu et al., 2019; Lin et al., 2020), we report model performance as measured in Accuracy (ACC), Normalized Mutual Information (NMI; Strehl and Ghosh, 2002) and the Adjusted Rand Index (ARI; Steinley, 2004). For more in-depth explanations and for the formulas of all three metrics, please refer to Appendix C. All three metrics are normalized to $[0, 1]$, where higher values indicate better performance. Similarly, we use the Hungarian algorithm (Kuhn, 1955) to optimally map predicted labels to the true cluster assignments before calculating the performance metrics.

4 Experiments

In Table 2, we compare the CC models trained via both the MCL and the KCL loss with the lower and upper baselines. These results confirm that CC is a suitable method to train weakly supervised models for the detection of topics in short texts, reaching almost full supervision performance.

Furthermore, we investigated the capabilities of these models in the OC scenario, where the ground truth number of classes is unknown during training and the model can potentially assign $n_{out} = 30 >$

		Lower Baseline			CC-KCL			CC-MCL			Upper Baseline		
Data set	K	ACC	NMI	ARI	ACC	NMI	ARI	ACC	NMI	ARI	ACC	NMI	ARI
AG News	4	0.830	0.577	0.605	0.870	0.714	0.739	**0.917**	**0.755**	**0.795**	0.919	0.759	0.800
TREC-coarse	6	0.542	0.299	0.302	0.953	0.890	0.900	**0.967**	**0.908**	**0.923**	0.962	0.897	0.917
DBPedia	14	0.631	0.726	0.494	**0.982**	**0.963**	**0.967**	0.661	0.805	0.653	0.989	0.974	0.977

Table 2: Averaged results for the baselines on all available training samples as well as for CC-MCL and CC-KCL trained with $20,000$ constraints each. The better CC model (between KCL and MCL) is marked in bold and CC models almost reach full supervision level performance (upper baseline). Refer to a larger version of this table including standard deviations across runs in Appendix B, Table 6.

Dataset	ACC	NMI	ARI
AG News	0.821 ± 0.068	0.670 ± 0.033	0.677 ± 0.067
TREC coarse	0.912 ± 0.070	0.892 ± 0.057	0.882 ± 0.075
DBpedia	0.986 ± 0.002	0.966 ± 0.003	0.969 ± 0.003

Table 3: Mean results $\pm$ std. deviations over 5 repetitions for overclustering with $n_{out} = 30$. The model performs well despite the absence of the true K.

K potential clusters. From the results in Table 3, we observe that CC copes very well with this challenging scenario. This motivates the extension towards DTD.

Following Section 3.3, we train five *Phase 1* models $f_{i,t=1}$ on $D_{train,t=1}$ and evaluate their performance on the three different test sets using the DBPedia data set. We use the KCL loss due to its superior performance in the previous experiments. We observe a decent performance on $D_{test,1}$ along with a correctly detected number of classes in Table 4. Note, that we consider a class as 'detected' if the model assigns at least one percent of the respective test set to the specific cluster. We acknowledge that this is a rather heuristic choice. For $D_{test,2}$ and $D_{test,combined}$, the models perform substantially worse and are not able to detect the correct number of classes. Still, it is noteworthy, that the model is able to detect that the four novel classes in $D_{test,2}$ are distinct as it assigns them different clusters and does not simply assign them one 'outlier' cluster. From the observation that the model detects a total of ten clusters, as opposed to the correct $K = 14$ for $D_{test,combined}$, we infer that while it realizes these four new clusters are distinct, it assigns them to the clusters present in $D_{train,t=1}$. However, the *Phase 2* model $f_{t=2}$ obtained by fine-tuning the best performing *Phase 1* for 200 epochs on $10,000$ constraints sampled from $D_{train,t=2}$ (50% new vs. 50% old) performs very well on all three test sets and is able to detect the correct overall number of classes. Refer to the confusion matrices in Figure 2 for further illustration of these results. When $D_{train,t=2}$ contains more samples from the 'old' classes (25% new vs. 75% old), overall model performance still improves compared to *Phase 1*, but substantially less compared to when there is more information about the 'new' classes. These results imply that the algorithm shows considerable sensitivity to the degree of novelty present in the new training data, which has to be investigated further in future research. This experiment shows how an OC-KCL model can easily be adapted to a dynamically changing number of clusters via continued training on pairwise annotations from newly incoming training data.

5 Discussion and Conclusion

In this work, we connected two branches of research: contemporary NLP research and weakly supervised learning approaches. While the usefulness of CC-KCL (and MCL) had already been shown for computer vision settings (Hsu and Kira, 2016; Hsu et al., 2019), we extended it towards NLP. Based on this, we showcased how existing shortcomings of ordinary supervised approaches – the requirement of fixed, static label sets – could be regarded as a new type of learning task which we introduced as *dynamic topic discovery*. Within DTD, we subsume a dynamic setting where an initial, weakly annotated training data set at time $t = 1$ is accompanied by a second data set at time $t = 2$ which contains novel classes unseen at $t = 1$. We proposed a potential solution for such DTD settings via an alternative training scheme leveraging the overclustering and category detection capabilities of CC models. We acknowledge that there are still numerous unsolved problems such as the application on *very* short texts, *very* large label sets with large class cardinality, or multi-label scenarios. Nevertheless, we hope that our experimental results can serve as a foundation for further research toward tackling these increasingly complex problems to ultimately reduce manual labeling efforts in NLP.

	Test set	ACC		NMI		Predicted K	
Phase 1	$D_{test,1}$	**0.988** / 0.982 ± 0.009		**0.969** / 0.964 ± 0.005		10 (Range: $[10-10]$)	
(**Best** / Mean $\pm$ Std. Dev)	$D_{test,2}$	**0.616** / 0.570 ± 0.043		**0.409** / 0.410 ± 0.048		4 (Range: $[4-5]$)	
	$D_{test,combined}$	**0.717** / 0.710 ± 0.011		**0.809** / 0.808 ± 0.015		10 (Range: $[10-11]$)	
		50% new – 50% old			25% new – 75% old		
		ACC	NMI	Predicted K	ACC	NMI	Predicted K
Phase 2	$D_{test,1}$	0.980	0.951	10	0.880	0.895	9
	$D_{test,2}$	0.971	0.929	4	0.951	0.866	4
	$D_{test,combined}$	0.978	0.953	14	0.832	0.887	12

Table 4: DTD (with KCL) on DBpedia for different ratios of new versus old classes in $D_{train,t=2}$, from which we sample the 10,000 constraints for Phase 2, controlling the degree of novelty. Phase 1 is based on five different models on $D_{train,t=1}$. For Phase 2, we pick the best Phase 1 model and continue training on the constraints from $D_{train,t=2}$ (no standard deviations, since no random initialization of any model weights for Phase 2).

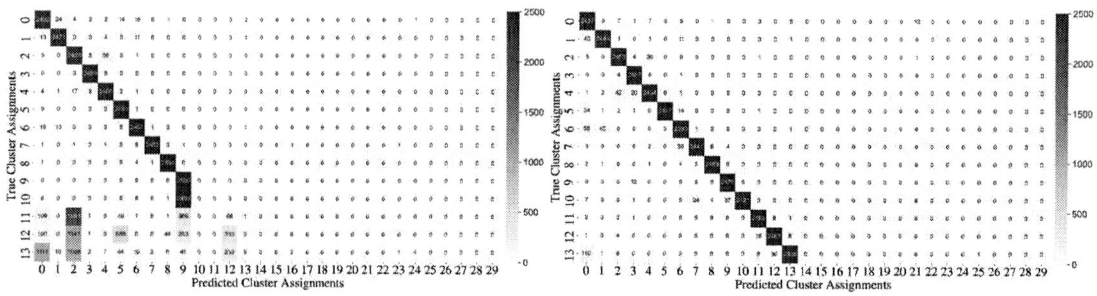

Figure 2: Confusion matrices for the two DTD phases on the $D_{test,combined}$. Phase 2 results (right) from the 50% new - 50% old setting illustrate a clear improvement over the results from Phase 1 (left). This shows that the Phase 2 model is able to cluster both the new and old data correctly.

Further, we believe that there is a high necessity for investigating DTD more in-depth. We believe it is important to design appropriate benchmarks and to investigate their relations to other dynamic paradigms, such as e.g. online learning or novel category discovery, and we hope this work can serve as a step in that direction.

Limitations

While we hope that this work provides valuable insights, there are still a couple of issues we did not yet address. First, we observed considerable instability during model training, especially for a lower number of constraints. Second, we found KCL to work better for DBpedia than MCL, which is surprising given the findings of Hsu et al. (2019). Finally, we (i) only evaluated DTD for one fixed set of constraints, (ii) only used the DBPedia dataset (due to the low number of classes in the other two datasets), and (iii) used a rather heuristic rule for determining the number of detected classes.

Acknowledgements

This work has been partially funded by the Deutsche Forschungsgemeinschaft (DFG, German Research Foundation) as part of BERD@NFDI - grant number 460037581. This work was supported by the Bavarian Ministry of Economic Affairs, Regional Development and Energy through the Center for Analytics – Data – Applications (ADACenter) within the framework of BAYERN DIGITAL II (20-3410-2-9-8).

References

David Arthur and Sergei Vassilvitskii. 2006. How slow is the k-means method? In *Proceedings of the twenty-second annual symposium on Computational geometry*, pages 144–153.

Francesco Barbieri, Jose Camacho-Collados, Luis Espinosa-Anke, and Leonardo Neves. 2020. TweetEval: Unified Benchmark and Comparative Evaluation for Tweet Classification. In *Proceedings of Findings of EMNLP*.

Sugato Basu, Arindam Banerjee, and Raymond J Mooney. 2004. Active semi-supervision for pairwise constrained clustering. In *Proceedings of the 2004*

SIAM international conference on data mining, pages 333–344. SIAM.

David M Blei, Andrew Y Ng, and Michael I Jordan. 2003. Latent dirichlet allocation. *Journal of machine Learning research*, 3(Jan):993–1022.

Scott Deerwester, Susan T Dumais, George W Furnas, Thomas K Landauer, and Richard Harshman. 1990. Indexing by latent semantic analysis. *Journal of the American society for information science*, 41(6):391–407.

Jacob Devlin, Ming-Wei Chang, Kenton Lee, and Kristina Toutanova. 2019. BERT: Pre-training of deep bidirectional transformers for language understanding. In *Proceedings of the 2019 Conference of the North American Chapter of the Association for Computational Linguistics: Human Language Technologies, Volume 1 (Long and Short Papers)*, pages 4171–4186, Minneapolis, Minnesota. Association for Computational Linguistics.

Pierre Gançarski, Thi-Bich-Hanh Dao, Bruno Crémilleux, Germain Forestier, and Thomas Lampert. 2020. Constrained clustering: Current and new trends. In *A Guided Tour of Artificial Intelligence Research*, pages 447–484. Springer.

Maarten Grootendorst. 2022. Bertopic: Neural topic modeling with a class-based tf-idf procedure. *arXiv preprint arXiv:2203.05794*.

Yen-Chang Hsu and Zsolt Kira. 2015. Neural network-based clustering using pairwise constraints. *arXiv preprint arXiv:1511.06321*.

Yen-Chang Hsu and Zsolt Kira. 2016. Neural network-based clustering using pairwise constraints. *ICLR Workshop*.

Yen-Chang Hsu, Zhaoyang Lv, and Zsolt Kira. 2018. Learning to cluster in order to transfer across domains and tasks. *ICLR*.

Yen-Chang Hsu, Zhaoyang Lv, Joel Schlosser, Phillip Odom, and Zsolt Kira. 2019. Multi-class classification without multi-class labels. In *7th International Conference on Learning Representations, ICLR 2019, New Orleans, LA, USA, May 6-9, 2019*.

Shaohan Huang, Furu Wei, Lei Cui, Xingxing Zhang, and Ming Zhou. 2020. Unsupervised fine-tuning for text clustering. In *Proceedings of the 28th International Conference on Computational Linguistics*, pages 5530–5534.

Harold W Kuhn. 1955. The hungarian method for the assignment problem. *Naval research logistics quarterly*, 2(1-2):83–97.

Ken Lang. 1995. Newsweeder: Learning to filter netnews. In *Machine Learning Proceedings 1995*, pages 331–339. Elsevier.

Jens Lehmann, Robert Isele, Max Jakob, Anja Jentzsch, Dimitris Kontokostas, Pablo N Mendes, Sebastian Hellmann, Mohamed Morsey, Patrick Van Kleef, Sören Auer, et al. 2015. Dbpedia–a large-scale, multilingual knowledge base extracted from wikipedia. *Semantic web*, 6(2):167–195.

Xin Li and Dan Roth. 2002. Learning question classifiers. In *COLING 2002: The 19th International Conference on Computational Linguistics*.

Ting-En Lin, Hua Xu, and Hanlei Zhang. 2020. Discovering new intents via constrained deep adaptive clustering with cluster refinement. In *Proceedings of the AAAI Conference on Artificial Intelligence*, volume 34, pages 8360–8367.

Ilya Loshchilov and Frank Hutter. 2019. Decoupled weight decay regularization. *International Conference on Learning Representations*.

Saif Mohammad, Svetlana Kiritchenko, Parinaz Sobhani, Xiaodan Zhu, and Colin Cherry. 2016. Semeval-2016 task 6: Detecting stance in tweets. In *Proceedings of the 10th International Workshop on Semantic Evaluation (SemEval-2016)*, pages 31–41.

Adam Paszke, Sam Gross, Soumith Chintala, Gregory Chanan, Edward Yang, Zachary DeVito, Zeming Lin, Alban Desmaison, Luca Antiga, and Adam Lerer. 2017. Automatic differentiation in pytorch. In *Proceedings of the 31st Conference on Neural Information Processing Systems (NIPS 2017), Workshops*, Long Beach, CA, USA.

Tim Schopf, Daniel Braun, and Florian Matthes. 2021. Lbl2vec: An embedding-based approach for unsupervised document retrieval on predefined topics. In *WEBIST*, pages 124–132.

Douglas Steinley. 2004. Properties of the hubert-arable adjusted rand index. *Psychological methods*, 9(3):386.

Alexander Strehl and Joydeep Ghosh. 2002. Cluster ensembles—a knowledge reuse framework for combining multiple partitions. *Journal of machine learning research*, 3(Dec):583–617.

Chi Sun, Xipeng Qiu, Yige Xu, and Xuanjing Huang. 2019. How to fine-tune bert for text classification? In *China national conference on Chinese computational linguistics*, pages 194–206. Springer.

Kiri Wagstaff and Claire Cardie. 2000. Clustering with instance-level constraints. *AAAI/IAAI*, 1097:577–584.

Thomas Wolf, Lysandre Debut, Victor Sanh, Julien Chaumond, Clement Delangue, Anthony Moi, Pierric Cistac, Tim Rault, Rémi Louf, Morgan Funtowicz, et al. 2020. Transformers: State-of-the-art natural language processing. In *Proceedings of the 2020 conference on empirical methods in natural language processing: system demonstrations*, pages 38–45.

Hanlei Zhang, Hua Xu, Ting-En Lin, and Rui Lyu. 2021a. Discovering new intents with deep aligned clustering. In *Proceedings of the AAAI Conference on Artificial Intelligence*, volume 35, pages 14365–14373.

Hongjing Zhang, Tianyang Zhan, Sugato Basu, and Ian Davidson. 2021b. A framework for deep constrained clustering. *Data Mining and Knowledge Discovery*, 35(2):593–620.

Xiang Zhang, Junbo Zhao, and Yann LeCun. 2015. Character-level convolutional networks for text classification. *Advances in neural information processing systems*, 28.

Appendix

A Training Model Configurations

In Table 5 we list the specifications of the BERT-based language model that we use as architectural backbone which we obtained via huggingface (Wolf et al., 2020). We implemented our models and data loading logic in PyTorch (Paszke et al., 2017). Model training for the constrained clustering and the overclustering experiments was done on an NVIDIA A100-SXM4-40GB GPU with a batch size of 256 for 200 epochs. The models for the DTD part were trained on an NVIDIA Tesla-V100-16GB GPU with a batch size of 196 for 100 training epochs for phase 1 and for 200 training epochs for phase 2.

Parameter	Value
Base model	BERT-BASE-UNCASED
Learning rate	1×10^{-5}
Optimizer	AdamW (Loshchilov and Hutter, 2019)
Adam Epsilon	1×10^{-8}

Table 5: BERT configurations for all experiments.

B Detailed Results

In Table 6, we show results for the constrained clustering experiments with $n_{out} = K$ and a total of 20.000 constraint annotations for model training for the three datasets. This table includes mean $\pm$ standard deviations for the performance metrics across 5 repeated training runs to account for randomness in the training process. The results show that constrained clustering offers a viable alternative to supervised learning, almost reaching the upper baseline performance for the three datasets. Further, the MCL loss works best for the AGNews and the TREC-coarse datasets whereas the KCL loss is more suitable for the DBPedia dataset. Hence, we used the KCL loss in the experiments on DBPedia for the dynamic topic discovery experiments in Section 3.3.

C Performance metrics

Normalized Mutual Information (NMI) NMI is generally used to measure the tightness of the cluster formations. In other words, it quantifies if all the clusters are mutually exclusive without outliers (Strehl and Ghosh, 2002). Mathematically,

		Lower Baseline		
Data set	K	ACC	NMI	ARI
AG News	4	0.830	0.577	0.605
TREC-coarse	6	0.542	0.299	0.302
DBPedia	14	0.631	0.726	0.494
		CC-KCL		
AG News	4	0.870 ± 0.088	0.714 ± 0.059	0.730 ± 0.087
TREC-coarse	6	0.953 ± 0.007	0.890 ± 0.010	0.900 ± 0.012
DBPedia	14	$\mathbf{0.982} \pm 0.005$	$\mathbf{0.963} \pm 0.005$	$\mathbf{0.967} \pm 0.009$
		CC-MCL		
AG News	4	$\mathbf{0.917} \pm 0.003$	$\mathbf{0.755} \pm 0.004$	$\mathbf{0.795} \pm 0.006$
TREC-coarse	6	$\mathbf{0.967} \pm 0.004$	$\mathbf{0.908} \pm 0.009$	$\mathbf{0.923} \pm 0.009$
DBPedia	14	0.661 ± 0.057	0.805 ± 0.038	0.653 ± 0.055
		Upper Baseline		
AG News	4	0.919 ± 0.001	0.759 ± 0.005	0.800 ± 0.003
TREC-coarse	6	0.962 ± 0.002	0.897 ± 0.006	0.917 ± 0.005
DBPedia	14	0.989 ± 0.001	0.974 ± 0.001	0.977 ± 0.001

Table 6: Results for the baselines on all available training samples for all of the analyzed data sets as well as for CC-MCL and CC-KCL on 20,000 constraints each. The better CC model (between KCL and MCL) is marked in bold. Mean and standard deviations of the metrics over five runs.

NMI describes the change in entropy of class labels given the true cluster labels:

$$NMI = \frac{2 \cdot I(Y, \hat{Y})}{H(Y) + H(\hat{Y})}$$

where $I(Y, \hat{Y}) = H(Y) - H(Y|\hat{Y})$ is the mutual information. $H(Y)$ and $H(\hat{Y})$ are the entropy of the ground truth class label Y distribution and the entropy of the predicted cluster label distribution $\hat{Y}$, respectively. The NMI is bound to $[0, 1]$ where a higher score implies better clustering performance.

Accuracy (ACC) Accuracy measures the similarity of predicted results with the respective ground truth. For clustering accuracy, we use the Hungarian algorithm (Kuhn, 1955) to assign predicted clusters with associated class labels. Given ground truth classes Y and predicted clusters $\hat{Y}$ we calculate accuracy as:

$$ACC = \frac{TP + TN}{TP + TN + FP + FN}$$

where TP is the number of true positives, TN is the number of true negatives, FP is the number of false positives, and FN is the number of false negatives.

Adjusted Rand Index (ARI) The ARI is used to measure the similarity between two clustering outputs (Steinley, 2004). Here, the actual class labels are compared to predicted cluster labels to measure the clustering performance. When comparing Y and $\hat{Y}$, the ARI is calculated as follows:

$$R = \frac{a + b}{\binom{n}{2}}$$

where a is the number of times, pairs of elements are in the same cluster for Y and $\hat{Y}$, b is the number of times a pair of elements is not in the same cluster for Y and $\hat{Y}$ and n is the total number of samples in the batch.

HSE at TempoWiC: Detecting Meaning Shift in Social Media with Diachronic Language Models

Elizaveta Tukhtina, Svetlana Vydrina, Kseniia Kashleva
HSE University
{eatukhtina, svvydrina, kkashleva}@edu.hse.ru

Abstract

This paper describes our methods for temporal meaning shift detection, implemented during the TempoWiC shared task. We present two systems: with and without time span data usage. Our approach is based on masked language models continuously pre-trained with Twitter data. Both systems outperformed all the competition's baselines except TimeLMs-SIM. Our best submission achieved the macro-F1 score of 70.09% and took the 7th place. This result was achieved by using diachronic language models from the TimeLMs project.

1 Introduction

It is a commonplace that words change their meanings and connotations through time. Despite numerous studies about that, there are still difficulties in semantic change detection. Static embeddings are not suitable for working with semantic change, since they cannot reflect the fact that a word can have completely unrelated meanings. In this work, we are focusing on contextualized embeddings, which produce different vector representations depending on the context.

There were a number of competitions dedicated to semantic change detection, for example, TempoWiC (Loureiro et al., 2022b) and LSCDiscovery (Kashleva et al., 2022). These competitions were aimed at determining the difference in the meanings of words depending on the time period in which they are used. Datasets at LSCDiscovery consisted of texts from different centuries (Zamora-Reina et al., 2022). For this shared task, TempoWiC, the data with a time interval only of one year is used. It significantly changes the approach to the competition.

Temporal word in context (TempoWiC) benchmark aims to decide if there is a change between the meaning of two words in a given pair of tweets. TempoWiC is designed as a binary classification problem where the target word is featured in two tweets from different time periods, and the goal is to detect whether there is a meaning shift or not.

When creating a dataset for the competition, the authors decided to use data from social media (Twitter), while when developing the previous dataset WiC (Pilehvar and Camacho-Collados, 2018), word usage was taken from more formal sources such as Wiktionary, WordNet and VerbNet. The language used in social networks is much more informal and dynamic, so such a dataset is able to reflect even minor changes in word usage.

The TempoWiC dataset consists of paired tweets and is divided into train/validation/test samples of size 1,428/396/1,473 instances, respectively. For each sample, the set of target words is different. As additional data, the publication date is indicated for each tweet. There are no missing values in the dataset. Participants of the competition were asked to detect the change in the meaning of the target word both with and without using time-span information. To estimate the system's performance, the Macro-F1 score was used.

2 Systems Overview

In this section, we describe two systems that were implemented by our team during the shared task. Both systems are based on the pre-trained language models. For our first system, we did not use time-span information and extracted embeddings from the Twitter-roBERTa-base model (Barbieri et al., 2020). In the second approach, we tried to improve our system's performance by using diachronic language models from the TimeLMs project (Loureiro et al., 2022a).

2.1 General approach

First, we apply the continual learning strategy and train a masked language model with the TempoWiC data, using the script provided by the HuggingFace

Proceedings of the The First Workshop on Ever Evolving NLP (EvoNLP), pages 35 - 38
December 7, 2022 ©2022 Association for Computational Linguistics

team[1]. Depending on the experiment, we use the entire dataset or a sub-set. In each experiment, we split a given corpus into train and test sets with a 95:5 ratio and train the model for 4 epochs with a learning rate of 2e-5. Then we extract summed representations for target words from all 12 layers of a corresponding language model. We decided to focus on word-level representations since they showed a better performance than sentence-level embeddings (see Appendix A for comparison results). For a word representation we adopt only the embedding of the first subword. Finally, we calculate cosine similarities between representations of two target words in each pair of tweets and use the obtained values to train a logistic regression model. Though the cosine-based approach is rather straightforward, its performance may strongly vary on the choice of the language model.

2.2 System 1. Twitter-roBERTa-base with additional pre-training

Our first system is based on the Twitter-roBERTa-base language model. It is a RoBERTa model (Liu et al., 2019) that was trained on 58M tweets. We chose this model because the competition's task was focused on Twitter data. For additional pre-training, we took all of the available tweets from the TempoWiC dataset, including train, validation, and test sets. For comparison, we also tried the BERT-base model (Devlin et al., 2018) as a baseline for our first system.

2.3 System 2. Diachronic models from the TimeLMs project

The distinguishing feature of the TempoWiC dataset is that each tweet has a specified time period: a year and a month when the tweet was posted. That means we can take into account not only the context of the tweet but also use time as an additional feature to improve our meaning shift detection system.

Our second solution is based on diachronic language models from the TimeLMs project. TimeLMs is a set of diachronic language models, based on RoBERTa, continuously trained on Twitter data over regular time intervals. The initial model was trained on tweets that were posted from 2018 until the end of 2019. Since the beginning of 2020, the base model has been continuously pre-training on diachronic Twitter data every three months. The project is active and at the time of this writing, models from 2019 to June 2022 are available. Since the TempoWiC dataset contains tweets from 2019, 2020, and 2021, models from the TimeLMs project can be applied to improve our first 'nondiachronic' approach.

For our baseline diachronic approach, we used three TimeLMs models trained on Twitter data for a specific year: 2019, 2020 and 2021. The choice of the diachronic model for extracting the representation of a target word depends on the tweet's publication year. We also split the TempoWiC dataset into three corpora by year and additionally pre-trained each of the TimeLMs models with the corresponding corpus.

As an improvement strategy, we also decided to engage the TimeLMs models from a year's quarters. In this case, the choice of the model depends on the year's quarter in which the tweet was posted. Due to the lack of quarterly models for 2019 and because the number of tweets for 2021 was insufficient for pre-training quarterly models, this improvement was applied only to the tweets from 2020. Table 1 lists all of the TimeLMs models that were used for our second system.

Time span	Model
01.2019-12.2019	twitter-roberta-base-2019-90m
01.2020-03.2020	twitter-roberta-base-mar2020
04.2020-06.2020	twitter-roberta-base-jun2020
07.2020-09.2020	twitter-roberta-base-sep2020
10.2020-12.2020	twitter-roberta-base-dec2020
01.2021-12.2021	twitter-roberta-base-2021-124m

Table 1: TimeLMs models used in System 2 in accordance with time spans for the tweets from the TempoWiC dataset.

3 Results

Table 3 shows the results for our two final systems. Submissions were evaluated using the Macro-F1 metric. Our best submission took 7th place. That is better than all baselines except TimeLMs-SIM (Logistic Regression based on Similarity of Contextual Embeddings from TimeLMs-2019-90M). This result is interesting because our best model (TimeLMs-with-quarter) seems more complex than the TimeLMs-SIM baseline, since we used a different model depending on the time span. According to the description of the baselines that became available after the evaluation phase, the task organiz-

[1] The script is available at `https://github.com/huggingface/transformers/blob/main/examples/pytorch/language-modeling/run_mlm.py`

Model	Validation (original LM)	Validation (LM with extra pre-training)	Test (original LM)	Test (LM with extra pre-training)
BERT-base-uncased	57.39	59.47	67.98	67.11
Twitter-RoBERTa-base	58.26	**67.61**	68.29	**68.76**
TimeLMs-by-year	57.50	66.63	63.81	68.69
TimeLMs-with-quarters	57.97	**68.70**	64.22	**70.09**

Table 2: Macro F1-scores for all of our models, including post-evaluation results for the Test set. Best results for Validation and Test sets are highlighted in bold.

ers used SP-WSD layer pooling weights (Loureiro et al., 2022d). Whereas in our system, we extracted summed embeddings from all 12 layers without pooling strategy.

Rank	User/Baseline	Submission 1 Macro-F1	Submission 2 Macro-F1
	Our results		
7	lisatukhtina	70.09	68.76
	TOP-3 results from other teams		
1	dma	77.05	77.05
2	macd	76.60	74.74
3	zackchen	73.64	74.87
	Baselines		
—	TimeLMs - SIM	70.33	
—	RoBERTa-L - SIM	67.09	
—	RoBERTa-L - FT	59.10	
—	TimeLMs - FT	57.70	
—	Random	50.00	
—	All True	26.79	

Table 3: Submission leaderboard

Table 2 shows detailed results for all the models we implemented during the shared task. For the validation set, there is a noticeable difference between the models with and without continued pre-training. We expected a similar trend for the test sample. To test this assumption, we obtained results for all our models in the post-evaluation phase. The results showed that for the BERT and Twitter-RoBERTa-base models, additional pre-training did not improve the quality on the test set. As for TimeLMs models, the results are correlated with the validation set. It is also interesting that such a general model as BERT-base performed as well as more complex solutions, even without pre-training for Twitter domain.

For the validation set, we also obtained Macro-F1 scores for each target word (see Table 4). The most challenging words for both models were *recount* and *primo*.

Word	Macro-F1 Twitter-RoBERTa-base	Macro-F1 TimeLMs
impostor	65.97	70.62
lotte	67.07	64.10
recount	52.88	61.86
primo	57.65	60.17

Table 4: Macro-F1 scores for each word from the validation set.

4 Discussion

The main question that is still open is that: can we really detect a meaning shift on such a short time period as about a year? At TempoWiC it was postulated that in social media we can observe faster semantic shifts (Loureiro et al., 2022c). From a linguistic point of view, a change occurred, when there is evidence of transmission of innovations to others, i.e., of conventionalization (Traugott, 2017). It seems that one year is too short time for any language innovation to become widespread, even via social media. Moreover, it may take more time to be sure that this is a real change and not a nonce word. Let us consider words that were taken for a validation set. There were 4 of them (*lotte*, *primo*, *recount*, and *impostor*). According to the corpus provided by the organizers, the word *recount* was mostly used in the context of elections, *lotte* in the context of a concert and as a hotel name. It means that at least 50% of validation words demonstrate that trending words in Twitter in general most likely describe ongoing or recent events.

It was said that at TempoWiC the task was to decide if the meaning of the first target word in context is the same as the second one or not (Loureiro et al., 2022c). There are also examples of annotated sentences with target words in the article (see Table 5). These examples demonstrate polysemy, not semantic change. So it can be assumed that the TempoWiC dataset is much more suitable for word sense disambiguation task than for semantic change detection. It is difficult to differentiate

Tweet 1	Tweet 2	Label
2019-08	2020-08	
"In case you were wondering facial devotion still worked with a face *mask* on"	"With these *mask* at work customers are forever confusing me and Reyna lmao"	1

Table 5: An example from the TempoWiC training set for a target word 'mask'. Label 1 indicates that the word has different meanings in the two tweets.

between polysemy and semantic change on such restricted data. That makes this shared task even more complicated.

5 Conclusion

We presented two systems for temporal meaning shift detection in Twitter, both with and without time span data usage. The best result was obtained with diachronic language models continuously trained for the Twitter domain. For our future research, we will consider weight-pooling methods as an attempt to improve our system's performance.

Acknowledgements

We deeply thank Lidia Pivovarova for her invaluable advice and help.

References

Francesco Barbieri, Jose Camacho-Collados, Luis Espinosa Anke, and Leonardo Neves. 2020. TweetEval: Unified benchmark and comparative evaluation for tweet classification. In *Findings of the Association for Computational Linguistics: EMNLP 2020*, pages 1644–1650, Online. Association for Computational Linguistics.

Jacob Devlin, Ming-Wei Chang, Kenton Lee, and Kristina Toutanova. 2018. Bert: Pre-training of deep bidirectional transformers for language understanding.

Kseniia Kashleva, Alexander Shein, Elizaveta Tukhtina, and Svetlana Vydrina. 2022. HSE at LSCDiscovery in Spanish: Clustering and profiling for lexical semantic change discovery. In *Proceedings of the 3rd Workshop on Computational Approaches to Historical Language Change*, pages 193–197, Dublin, Ireland. Association for Computational Linguistics.

Yinhan Liu, Myle Ott, Naman Goyal, Jingfei Du, Mandar Joshi, Danqi Chen, Omer Levy, Mike Lewis, Luke Zettlemoyer, and Veselin Stoyanov. 2019. Roberta: A robustly optimized bert pretraining approach.

Daniel Loureiro, Francesco Barbieri, Leonardo Neves, Luis Espinosa Anke, and Jose Camacho-Collados. 2022a. Timelms: Diachronic language models from twitter.

Daniel Loureiro, Aminette D'Souza, Areej Nasser Muhajab, Isabella A. White, Gabriel Wong, Luis Espinosa Anke, Leonardo Neves, Francesco Barbieri, and Jose Camacho-Collados. 2022b. TempoWiC: An evaluation benchmark for detecting meaning shift in social media.

Daniel Loureiro, Aminette D'Souza, Areej Nasser Muhajab, Isabella A. White, Gabriel Wong, Luis Espinosa Anke, Leonardo Neves, Francesco Barbieri, and José Camacho-Collados. 2022c. Tempowic: An evaluation benchmark for detecting meaning shift in social media. *ArXiv*, abs/2209.07216.

Daniel Loureiro, Alípio Mário Jorge, and Jose Camacho-Collados. 2022d. LMMS reloaded: Transformer-based sense embeddings for disambiguation and beyond. *Artificial Intelligence*, 305:103661.

Mohammad Taher Pilehvar and Jose Camacho-Collados. 2018. Wic: the word-in-context dataset for evaluating context-sensitive meaning representations.

Elizabeth Closs Traugott. 2017. Semantic change.

Frank D. Zamora-Reina, Felipe Bravo-Marquez, and Dominik Schlechtweg. 2022. Lscdiscovery: A shared task on semantic change discovery and detection in spanish.

A Sentence-Level Representations

Table 6 presents the comparison results for word-level and sentence-level representations. Since the sentence-level embeddings showed poor performance for the Twitter-RoBERTa-base model (with Macro-F1 of 0.3613), we chose the word-level approach.

Model	Macro-F1 Sentence-level	Macro-F1 Word-level
BERT-base-uncased	56.33	57.39
Twitter-RoBERTa-base	36.13	58.26

Table 6: Comparison of sentence-level and word-level representations. Macro-F1 scores for Validation set.

Leveraging time-dependent lexical features for offensive language detection

Barbara McGillivray
King's College London &
The Alan Turing Institute
barbara.mcgillivray@kcl.ac.uk

Malithi Alahapperuma
Independent Researcher
malithi.alahapperuma@gmail.com

Jonathan Cook
University of Oxford
jonathan.cook2@eng.ox.ac.uk

Chiara Di Bonaventura
King's College London
chiara.di_bonaventura@kcl.ac.uk

Albert Meroño-Peñuela
King's College London
albert.merono@kcl.ac.uk

Gareth Tyson
Hong Kong University of
Science and Technology (GZ)
gtyson@ust.hk

Steven R. Wilson
Oakland University
stevenwilson@oakland.edu

Abstract

We present a study on the integration of time-sensitive information in lexicon-based offensive language detection systems. Our focus is on Offenseval sub-task A, aimed at detecting offensive tweets. We apply a semantic change detection algorithm over a short time span of two years to detect words whose semantics has changed and we focus particularly on those words that acquired or lost an offensive meaning between 2019 and 2020. Using the output of this semantic change detection approach, we train an Support Vector Machine (SVM) classifier on the Offenseval 2019 training set. We build on the already competitive SINAI system submitted to Offenseval 2019 by adding new lexical features, including those that capture the change in usage of words and their association with emerging offensive usages. We discuss the challenges, opportunities and limitations of integrating semantic change detection in offensive language detection models. Our work draws attention to an often neglected aspect of offensive language, namely that the meanings of words are constantly evolving and that NLP systems that account for this change can achieve good performance even when not trained on the most recent training data.

1 Introduction

The task of automatic detection of offensive language has attracted considerable attention in the Natural Language Processing (NLP) community recently. Policy makers and online platforms can leverage computational methods of offensive language detection to oppose online abuse and online harm at scale. These methods can also support computational social science and linguistics research in identifying innovative ways in which individuals and groups express offense online (Garland et al., 2020). The last two editions of the OffensEval shared task, organised as part of the SemEval competition, have offered a platform for assessing the state of the art in this area. Existing methods for automatic offensive language detection have been tested on a different large-scale annotated datasets, most notably the Offensive Language Identification Dataset (OLID) used in OffensEval 2019 (Zampieri et al., 2019a) and the Semi-Supervised Offensive Language Identification Dataset (SOLID) from OffensEval 2020 (Rosenthal et al., 2020).

The most effective methods proposed so far typically rely on ensembles of very large transformer-based language models such as BERT (Devlin et al., 2019) and its successors RoBERTa (Liu et al., 2019) and ALBERT (Lan et al., 2019). For example, Wiedemann et al. (2020), the top performing team for the offensive language detection task at OffensEval 2020, use tweets from SOLID to fine-tune the masked language modeling objective of BERT-like models before training them on the labeled OLID data for the task of offensive language

Proceedings of the The First Workshop on Ever Evolving NLP (EvoNLP), pages 39 - 54
December 7, 2022 ©2022 Association for Computational Linguistics

detection. Other systems (e.g. Arslan (2020) for Turkish) rely on more tailored sets of features such as existing lexicons of offensive words.

In spite of the growing amount of work on this topic, little attention has been devoted to more sophisticated uses of lexical features and on the role of the time dimension in offensive language phenomena. Languages are subject to constant change and their lexicons are no exception. Over time, words can acquire new meanings, or change or lose existing ones (Koptjevskaja-Tamm, 2002). These changes in the semantic profile of a word can take various shapes. For example, they can widen or narrow its semantic scope or change its polarity. An example is *sick*, which gained a positive connotation of 'excellent, impressive; risky' (OED Online) in slang contexts in the early 1980s. Lexical semantic change is a highly complex phenomenon and its study helps us better understand the relation between language and social, cultural and historical factors, and how this relation changes over time. This has important consequences for all computational systems that rely on word lists as input, including those used in offensive language detection systems, as such lists tend to be static and therefore do not account for the changes that words are subject to.

This paper focuses on the task of offensive language detection and follows the framework set up in the Offenseval 2019 and 2020 competitions, particularly subtask A. We build on SINAI (Plaza-del Arco et al., 2019), the only lexicon-based system submitted to Offenseval 2019 for which we could access the code. Our system relies on a set of refined lexical features which cover the surface-level spelling of offensive content as well as their semantic change over a short time period. Our system is aware of the change in meaning of the word *Karen*, for example, which, according to Dictionary.com, in 2020 acquired an offensive meaning.[1] Our work shows that accounting for language change and more sophisticated lexical features can help research in offensive language detection. At the same time, we show that detecting semantic changes that occurred in a very short time interval (one year in our case) presents challenges because this phenomenon affects a small number of words. Focusing on offensive language (and therefore on words whose semantics changed towards or away from an offensive meaning) presents additional challenges, as this phenomenon affects an even smaller number of words. Our results are promising, especially considering that they are obtained by drawing on lexical features from datasets covering only two consecutive years, the only years for which the Offenseval training and test sets are available. During this period, only a small number of words changed their meaning or polarity. Therefore, we expect our method to have a bigger impact when tested on a larger time span. We stress that one important methodological strength of our method is that it does not need an up-to-date training set. Because it uses an older annotated dataset as its training set, it enables significant savings in the human effort and computational resources needed to create high-quality labelled data, while still being able to handle the ever-evolving lexical semantics of offensive language.

In addition to presenting a manually curated list of words that acquired or lost an offensive meaning between 2019 and 2020, we perform an extensive error analysis to explore the categories of texts that are misclassified by our system. We find that further improvements will likely come from better contextual representations: these will help prevent cases in which models detect offense in any text that contains a word that *might* be offensive in certain contexts. We suggest expanding the current set of offensive words will help to correctly label cases in which rare but offensive words are used.

2 Related work

2.1 Offensive language detection

There has been extensive work on offensive language detection, with a particular focus on platforms such as Twitter (Davidson et al., 2017; Lee et al., 2018; Founta et al., 2018); Reddit (Mittos et al., 2020; Hada et al., 2021; Ribeiro and Silva, 2019) and YouTube (Ottoni et al., 2018). Researchers have experimented with a range of classification models that strive to identify offensive language automatically. Early work relied on established machine learning techniques such as logistic regression (Waseem and Hovy, 2016) and SVMs (Karan and Šnajder, 2018). Researchers have also developed deep learning models to detect abusive language, e.g., using Convolutional Neural networks (Gambäck and Sikdar, 2017; Ribeiro

[1] "Karen is a pejorative slang term for an obnoxious, angry, entitled, and often racist middle-aged white woman who uses her privilege to get her way or police other people's behaviors" `https://www.dictionary.com/e/slang/karen/`.

and Silva, 2019), Gated Recurrent Unit networks (Zhang et al., 2018) and Long short-term memory models (Badjatiya et al., 2017), as well as ensemble architectures of neural with non-neural models (Anand et al., 2022). Recent large pre-trained language models have led researchers to experiment with transfer learning approaches (El-Alami et al., 2022; Guest et al., 2021; Sohn and Lee, 2019; Polignano et al., 2019). For example, Mozafari et al. (2019) fine-tune a pre-trained BERT model for hate speech detection, gaining F1-score of 88% and 92% on two datasets (Waseem et al., 2017; Davidson et al., 2017). The efficacy of BERT-based techniques has been evidenced in various competitions (Zampieri et al., 2019b, 2020).

One issue of the aforementioned classification approaches is that they need large and up-to-date annotated datasets for model training. To address this issue in offensive language detection, Singh and Li (2021) propose a domain adaptation training for bidirectional transformers to enhance the detection performance on a target dataset by exploiting an external dataset. However, this approach has three main limitations: 1) target and auxiliary datasets might not share the same label space, resulting in ad-hoc data transformations; 2) an external large-scale dataset relevant to the target task is still needed; and 3) adding time-independent information does not remove the need for up-to-date annotated datasets. Indeed, language is subject to constant change: new words emerge all the time to refer to new concepts, for example, and existing words acquire new meanings (or lose their existing ones), a phenomenon that affects mainly open-class items (nouns, verbs, adjectives and adverbs), including offensive terms. By introducing a semantic change module, our work leverages time-dependent lexical features for offensive language detection which, in turn, could lighten the burden on having large-scale and up-to-date data.

2.2 Lexical semantic change detection

Over the past 15 years, the area of lexical semantic change detection has attracted a growing level of attention (Tahmasebi et al., 2018; Kutuzov et al., 2022). This task aims at identifying which words changed their meaning in a given time period. Researchers have proposed a range of methods to address this, from graph-based models (Mitra et al., 2015; Tahmasebi and Risse, 2017) to topic models (Cook et al., 2014; Lau et al., 2014; Frermann and Lapata, 2016), but the most successful methods involve type or token word embeddings (Kim et al., 2014; Basile and McGillivray, 2018; Kulkarni et al., 2015; Hamilton et al., 2016; Dubossarsky et al., 2017; Tahmasebi, 2018; Rudolph and Blei, 2018; Jatowt et al., 2018; Tang, 2018).

The most common approach to lexical semantic change detection consists in building type or token embedding representations of the semantics of words from an input diachronic corpus, which is split into subcorpora covering different time intervals. If type embeddings are used, these need to be aligned over the temporal sub-corpora, usually via orthogonal Procrustes (Hamilton et al., 2016), vector initialisation (Kim et al., 2014) or temporal referencing (Dubossarsky et al., 2019). Finally, significant shifts which can be interpreted as indications of semantic change are detected by measuring the change between the representations of the same word over time. This is typically done via distance metrics based on cosine or local neighbours.

In 2020 the first standard evaluation framework and dataset for this task were created for the SemEval 2020 shared task on Unsupervised lexical semantic change detection (Schlechtweg et al., 2020). The best-performing systems in this task use type embedding models, although the quality of the results differs depending on the language. Averaging over all four languages, the best result had an accuracy of 0.687 for sub-task 1 and a Spearman correlation coefficient of 0.527 for sub-task 2.

3 Approach

3.1 Overview

We experimented with enriching a lexicon-based offensive language detection system (OLD) with time-sensitive lexical features derived from lexical semantic change detection (LSCD) in a new system which we called LSCD+OLD. The idea behind this is to rely on "dated" manually annotated data to train a classifier that can label new instances of text for its offensiveness. Imagine that we have data annotated in 2019 (e.g. the OLID dataset) and we are interested in detecting offensive language in 2020. We expect that most of the words have not changed their meaning between 2019 and 2020, but some have, and a portion of those have acquired (or lost) an offensive meaning. These new meanings will not be recorded in the 2019 data and therefore our classifier is likely to miss instances of offensive texts if they contain one or

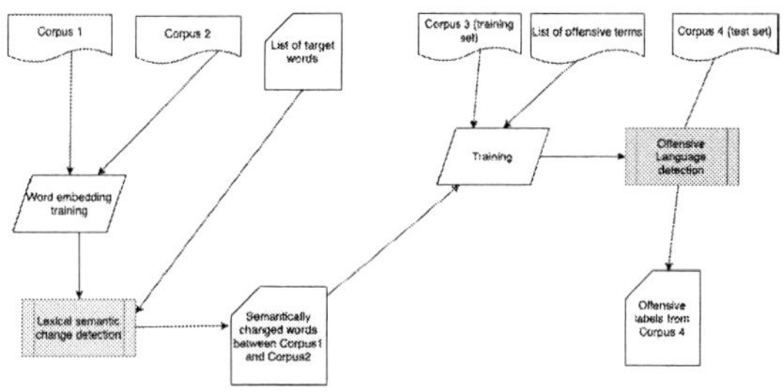

Figure 1: Diagram of our system, with the Semantic Change Detection (left) and the Offensive Language Detection (right) modules.

more of these words. We propose to overcome this by incorporating semantic change knowledge into the system. This means that we would not need to engage in the expensive process of producing new manually annotated data from 2020. Figure 1 shows the architecture of our system and the next sections describe its modules. The two modules are joined by a series of features that use the output of the LSCD module as input to the OLD classifier. Our code is available at `https://github.com/alan-turing-institute/offenseval-semantic-change`.

3.2 Lexical semantic change detection module

The *LSCD module* (left hand side of Figure 1) takes as input two corpora, representing the first time period t_1 (typically the time period when the manually annotated dataset was produced, 2019 in our case) and the second time period t_2 (the time after the manually annotated dataset was produced, 2020 in our case), respectively. Word embeddings are trained on the two corpora. For every target word in the intersection between the two vocabularies, the LSCD module outputs a semantic change score, representing the degree by which the word has changed between t_1 and t_2.

We chose UWB (Pražák et al., 2020) for the implementation of the LSCD module. UWB ranked first in sub-task 1 of SemEval 2020's shared task on unsupervised lexical semantic change detection, with an absolute accuracy of 0.687, which was the best result on average over all four languages (English, German, Latin, and Swedish). UWB involves training word embeddings for each of the two time-separated corpora, setting up two semantic vector spaces. Canonical Correlation Analysis, using the implementation from Brychcin et al. (2019) and a modification of the Orthogonal Transformation from VecMap (Artetxe et al., 2018) are then used to compute a linear transformation between the earlier and later spaces. Finally, the cosine distance between the transformed vector for the target word from the earlier corpus and the vector for the target word in the later corpus is measured and presented as the semantic change score. UWB's system consists of the following adjustable hyperparameters, with which we experimented with: (i) *Embedding dimensions*: the dimensions of the continuous vector space onto which the learned word representations are translated; (ii) *Window size*: the number of adjacent words used to determine the context of each word; (iii) *Iterations*: the number of times parameters are updated; (iv) *Minimum frequency count*: the minimum frequency below which uncommon words are set to unknown; and (v) *Maximum links*: the maximum number of links, i.e. size of vocabulary.

3.3 Offensive language detection module

The lexicon-based *OLD module* takes as input a training set and a list of offensive terms, which are used to train a classifier that can label a new set of texts as offensive or not. A description of the datasets is given in Section 4. The offensive language detection component of the proposed system is based on SINAI, developed by Plaza-del Arco et al. (2019) for SemEval-2019 Task 6: Identifying and Categorizing Offensive Language in Social Media (OffensEval). SINAI uses OLID data for training and testing and was the only lexicon-based system for which we could find the underlying code and were able to reproduce the Offenseval 2019 results. SINAI was chosen because the description of the other lexicon-based systems available in the corresponding system description papers for the Offenseval shared task were not sufficiently detailed to ensure that our implementation would have led to the same results as the original systems.

The system preprocesses the OLID data to remove mentions and URLs, and tokenize the tweets. It then trains a Support Vector Machine (SVM) classifier on *statistical features* (specifically TF-IDF scores) and the following two *lexical features*. (1) *Sentiment*: vaderSentiment[2] is used to obtain a vector with four scores: negative, positive, neutral, and compound polarity; and (2) *Offensive word list*: the proportion of tokens in the Offensive/Profane Word List[3] out of all tokens in each

[2] `https://pypi.org/project/vaderSentiment/`

[3] `https://www.cs.cmu.edu/~biglou/`

Table 1: Summary of OLID and SOLID datasets

Dataset	Tweets in training set	Tweets in test set
OLID	13,240	860
SOLID	6,209,964	3,887

tweet. In addition to SINAI's original features, we introduce three additional lexical features, a time-independent one and two time-dependent ones. The effect of introducing the time-dependent ones is that they consider the semantic change that affected words between 2019 and 2020 and therefore allow the classifier to "update" the 2019 training set.

Character length: For each tweet, the average number of characters of its tokens if they are contained in a offensive word list; this is based on the fact that many highly offensive words in English are short (typically four characters) (Bergen, 2016).

Polarity change: for every token found in both the 2019 and the 2020 corpora, we calculate the proportion of negative-sentiment tweets the token occurred in out of all tweets it occurred in. We calculate the difference between these two proportions and divide it by the 2019 proportion, to obtain the token's rate of change in proportion of negative tweets over time. For every tweet, we take the maximum polarity change value of all its tokens.

Sentiment and semantic change scores: for each token we multiply its semantic change score by its polarity change score as defined in the Polarity change features, and take the maximum value. This way, we aim to capture those words which underwent usage change and polarity change combined, with the idea to approximate the detection of those words that not only changed semantically, but whose semantics changed in an offensive direction.

4 Data

We rely on the OLID training dataset, which includes 13,240 tweets from late 2018 and 2019 annotated according to a three-layer hierarchical annotation scheme. The first layer identifies a tweet as containing offensive language (OFF) or not (NOT). The second layer categorizes the offensive language in tweets as a targeted insult (TIN) or an untargeted insult (UNT). The third layer categorises the targets of insults as an individual (IND), a group (GRP), or other (OTH) (Zampieri et al., 2019a). The OLID test set includes tweets categorized according to the sub-tasks, along with their gold labels. The offensive language detection system of our model uses the OLID training set for sub-task A.

resources/

SOLID contains tweet IDs for over 9,000,000 tweets from early 2020, also annotated according to the three-level hierarchy of OLID. We extract the content of over 6,000,000 tweets using the Twitter API by matching the SOLID tweet IDs. Contrary to the OLID dataset, SOLID does not contain gold standard labels for any of the sub-tasks. Instead, SOLID uses a democratic co-training method to provide the average confidence (AVG_CONF) and standard deviation from the AVG_CONF (CONF_STD) values of a particular tweet belonging to the positive class of that sub-task. For sub-task A, a tweet belongs to the positive class if it is labelled as offensive, or OFF (Rosenthal et al., 2020). We utilise a similar method as that used by Plaza del Arco et al. (2020) to generate the tweet labels using the AVG_CONF and CONF_STD values. We take 0.5 to be the threshold value for a tweet to be labelled offensive. If, for a given tweet, the AVG_CONF + CONF_STD value is still below the threshold value of 0.5, we label the tweet as NOT. If the AVG_CONF - CONF_STD gives a value more than the threshold, we label the tweet as OFF. Any tweets whose AVG_CONF + CONF_STD values were greater than 0.5, or AVG_CONF - CONF_STD values were less than 0.5 are discarded, as this indicates the OFF/NOT classification is not strongly established, and varies based on the standard deviation.

Table 1 gives a summary of the OLID and SOLID datasets. Following Plaza-del Arco et al. (2019), we preprocess the OLID and SOLID datasets by tokenizing the tweets using NLTK, lower-casing all tokens and removing URLs and Twitter user mentions.

4.1 Twitter corpora

In order to collect Twitter data from several years in the past, we download samples collected by the Archive Team.[4] These samples are taken from the Twitter 1% streaming API from 2012 until the time of the present study. We use only a small portion of this dataset from each year in order to keep the training time of the semantic change model manageable. We select a sample from the same time of each year (beginning of March). We obtain an average of 114,995 tweets for each year. More

[4]https://archive.org/details/twitterstream

Table 2: Summary of Twitter data sample to be used for LSCD module.

Year	Tweets	Tokens
2019	226,275	2,624,412
2012-2019	919,965	8,391,550
2020	364,708	4,205,419

statistics about the dataset can be found in Table 2.

We remove URLs, Twitter handles, and punctuation marks, and apply lower-casing. We correct cases in which the same character is repeated in a string (e.g. *faaast* vs. *fast*). We also lemmatise the text and exclude strings with fewer than three characters, with the exception of a fixed list of function words like pronouns and prepositions. Finally, we replace emoji with corresponding text using the emoji[5] Python package and tokenize using the Twitter tokenizer in NLTK (Bird et al., 2009). This last step was taken to simplify the data processing. However, we recognise that replacing emoji with their names will not capture the semantic change of emoji themselves, which we have investigated in one of our previous studies (Robertson et al., 2021). In future work we could look into incorporating these changes into our system.

4.2 Ground truth for semantic change

We compile a list of words for the evaluation of the LSCD module. These words not only changed their semantics between 2019 and 2020 but also did so by acquiring a new offensive meaning. We analyse a mix of online sources in order to identify offensive words whose definitions shifted between 2011 and 2019: Hatebase, an online repository of words associated with hate speech, and earlier academic offensive language lists, namely those by Luis von Ahn (Horta Ribeiro et al., 2018),[6] and by ElSherief et al. (2018b,a).[7]

We search Urban Dictionary[8] and `Dictionary.com` to confirm definitions and dates of meaning change. The criterion for selecting words from previously compiled lists was that they had to display at least one non-offensive and one offensive definition. We rely on Urban Dictionary, a crowd-sourced slang language dictionary, to verify definitions and to approximate the date at which a change occurred. We then search Dictionary.com's slang definition list of almost 1,000 words and phrases to find new negative connotations to existing words.

Lexical semantic change over a short time period such as the one considered here is a low-frequency phenomenon. Moreover, lexical semantic change involving a new offensive sense, which emerges alongside the established non-offensive senses, is an even rarer phenomenon. For this reason, the list had to be further refined to make sure that the corpora at our disposal displayed evidence of the words having undergone this phenomenon.

For example, *beta* occurs 49 times in the 2019 Twitter corpus and 67 times in the 2020 Twitter corpus. In 2019 the majority of its usages refer to the neutral software-related meaning reported by the Oxford English Dictionary as "a test of machinery, software, etc. in course of final development, carried out by a party or parties unconnected with the developer" (bet, 2021) as in (1) and none of the 2019 usages are offensive. On the other hand, the 2020 data show eight offensive usages out of 56 of "a slang insult for or describing a man who is seen as passive, subservient, weak, and effeminate",[9] as in (2):

(1) RTL Release 0.2.16-beta New Feature: Routing Peers - Routing history analysis by Peers (requested by @USER)

(2) Jelly viagra these man r so beta

For each of the selected words, we conduct a diachronic corpus analysis to check that the word was used in an offensive sense more often in the 2020 corpus than in the 2019 corpus. Through this, we obtain a subset of 21 lemmas. For each of these 21 lemmas we search for a corresponding stable lemma which did not acquire a new sense in 2020 (as checked against the Oxford English Dictionary) and which had similar frequency counts in the 2019 and 2020 corpus and same part of speech. In Appendix A, Table 7 shows the final list of 42 lemmas and Table 8 shows the list of positive gold standard words, i.e. the words that acquired an offensive meaning. The gold standard words are: *beta, canceled, cap, cringe, fag, globalist, karen, monkey, mug, ratchet, salty, simp, skip, snowflake, sus, thirsty, illegal, chad, gammon, Brexiter, triggered.* Appendix A contains additional information about their semantics.

[5] `https://pypi.org/project/emoji/`

[6] `https://github.com/manoelhortaribeiro/HatefulUsersTwitter/blob/master/data/extra/bad_words.txt`

[7] `https://github.com/mayelsherif/hate_speech_icwsm18/blob/master/hate_keywords.txt`

[8] `https://www.urbandictionary.com/`

[9] `https://www.dictionary.com/e/slang/beta/`

5 Experiments

In this section, we present the experiments performed to find the best configuration of parameters for our system.

5.1 Experimental setup

Our aim is to assess whether it is possible to train an OLD system on older data and achieve comparable performance when using this system to classify newer data. Therefore, we use the OLID training dataset as our training set, and the SOLID test set as our test set. During the development phase we could not use a portion of the OLID training set because its content is not from the same time period covered by SOLID. Therefore, we use a portion of SOLID as development — 0.2% of its data, corresponding to 9,915 tweets. We train the linear SVM classification algorithm (SVC) with C parameter 0.5 on SINAI's original features and also experiment with the additional lexical features we introduced in section 3.3.

Semantic change detection As part of the LSCD module of our system, we run the UWB code on two sets of corpora: Twitter 2019 vs. Twitter 2020; and Twitter 2012-2019 vs. Twitter 2020. Even though the time periods covered by OLID and SOLID are 2019 and 2020, respectively, we also want to see whether expanding the time period further back helps the performance.

Word embedding training As an input, we train word type embeddings with the following parameters: embedding dimensions: 100, 300, 1000; window size: 2, 5, 10; iterations: 5; min freq count: 1, 5, 10, 50, 100; embedding type: fasttext and word2vec; and embedding algorithm: skipgram and continuous-bags-of-words

Change detection We run the UWB code for the LSCD module of our system. We then train the SVC classifier on the features listed in section 3.3, setting three values for the threshold on the semantic change score: 0.5, 0.7, and 0.9.

5.2 Results

Our best model uses von Ahn's list of offensive words, the features described in Section 3.3 plus the TF-IDF features and SINAI's lexical featurxes, but not SINAI's sentiment features. The best system is based on the following parameters for the LSCD module: t_1 = 2019 and t_2 = 2020, word2vec embeddings with the continuous bag of words algorithm, 1000 dimensions, 5 iterations, a context window of 10, a minimum frequency count of 10 and 100000 maximum number of links used by the UWB code.

The output of the LSCD code is the list of the vocabulary words, paired with a lexical semantic change score. The higher the score the higher the likelihood that the word underwent lexical semantic change. In order to obtain a list of candidates for semantic change, a threshold must be set for the score: all words with a score above the threshold are then considered as candidates. We evaluate the LSCD module against the gold standard described in Section 4.2. True positives (TP) are the words that are identified as having undergone semantic change and that also appear in the gold standard set of changed words. True negatives (TN) are the words that are identified as not having changed and also appear in the gold standard set of unchanged words. False positives (FP) are the words that are identified as having changed but are in the gold standard list of unchanged words. False negatives (FN) are the words that are identified as not having changed but are in the gold standard list of changed words. Accuracy is calculated as $(TP + TN)/(TP + FP + TN + FN)$. Precision is calculated as $TP/(TP + FP)$ and recall as $TP/(TP + FN)$.

Table 3 shows the results. Table 4 shows an

Table 3: Evaluation results of the lexical semantic change module against our gold standard by different threshold values applied to the semantic change scores. The fifth row shows the number of words in the positive gold standard set that were also found as positive candidates for semantic change.

Metric	0.4	0.5	0.6	0.7	0.8	0.9
F1	0.93	0.93	0.57	0.42	0.24	0.24
Acc	0.89	0.92	0.64	0.58	0.50	0.50
Prec	1.00	1.00	1.00	1.00	1.00	1.00
Rec	0.87	0.87	0.40	0.27	0.13	0.13
#GS words	12	12	6	4	2	0

Table 4: Results of the quantitative comparison between the lexical semantic change output and the positive gold standard words.

Metric	Value
average score (positive gold standard)	0.60
median score (positive gold standard)	0.59
average score (other words)	0.49
median score (other words)	0.52
Mann-Whitney statistic	87631
Mann-Whitney p-value	0.02

Table 5: Results of experiments on the OffensEval 2020 test set; all systems were trained on the OLID training set (2019), apart from the last one, which was trained on SOLID (2020).

	SINAI	LSCD+OLD	SINAI
Training Data	*OLID*	*OLID*	SOLID
Test Data	SOLID	SOLID	SOLID
Precision (NOT)	0.97	0.97	**0.99**
Recall (NOT)	0.91	**0.92**	0.90
Prec. (OFF)	0.79	**0.82**	0.79
Recall (OFF)	0.93	0.93	**0.98**
Prec. (Macro)	0.88	**0.90**	0.89
Prec. (Weighted)	0.92	0.93	**0.94**
Recall (Macro)	0.92	0.93	**0.94**
Recall (Weighted)	0.91	**0.92**	**0.92**
Accuracy	0.91	**0.92**	**0.92**
F1 (Macro)	0.90	**0.91**	**0.91**

additional analysis aimed at measuring the output against the gold standard by comparing the average and median lexical semantic change score of the positive gold standard words and of the other words. Tables 3 and 4 show that the algorithm's performance with a threshold of 0.5 (the threshold chosen for the final model) is very good, even better than the current state-of-the-art from the SemEval 2020 task 1 results, where UWB achieved an average accuracy of 0.687 on the four languages and 0.622 on English. The setup of that shared task was very different to this study, as the English dataset covered a much longer time span (t_1 =1810–1860 and t_2 =1960–2010). Table 4 shows that the set of positive gold standard words have a significantly higher semantic change score compared with the other words, with an average of 0.60 vs. 0.49 and a median of 0.59 vs. 0.52, respectively.

Table 5 shows how our system compares to the original SINAI system trained on OLID and on its version trained on SOLID. The three system's performances are generally quite close to each other, with small differences. Our system combining extra general and time-dependent lexical features into SINAI performs better than the baseline in all metrics apart from the precision on the NOT class where it achieves the same results as the baseline.

It is interesting to note that our system achieved a macro-averaged F1 score of 0.94 on the development set drawn from 0.02% of the SOLID training set. This result may be explained by the fact that a larger set is more likely to capture a higher number of words that acquired an offensive meaning between 2019 and 2020, since this is a low-frequency phenomenon as we have seen. This suggests that our system may achieve even better performance when tested against a larger time span than the one-year period studied here.

6 Error analysis

In order to gain a better understanding of the 297 errors made by our proposed system, we qualitatively inspected the misclassified examples and sorted them into seven major categories (summarized in Table 6). Each misclassified instance was categorized by two of the authors. We calculated the Inter-Annotator Agreement (IAA) as Cohen's $\kappa = \frac{\sum a - \sum ef}{N - \sum ef}$, where $\sum a$ is the number of agreements, $\sum ef$ is the sum of the expected frequencies of agreement by chance, and N is the the number of misclassified instances (Cohen, 1960). We interpreted the IAA scores according to the following criteria: 0.01-0.20 points to no agreement/ slight agreement, 0.21-0.40 to fair agreement, 0.41-0.60 to moderate agreement, 0.61-0.80 to substantial agreement, and 0.81-1.00 to strong agreement. The average of the pairwise agreement is moderate (0.46), see Table 9 in Appendix A. This shows that the task is quite difficult, even for human annotators.

To present the analysis of the distribution of the seven categories we identified in the list of errors, we focus on 178 errors whose classification the two annotators agreed on. For examples that were misclassifed as offensive, the most common feature was the presence of offense-related words that were not being used in an offensive way. Models based solely on lexical features that do not account for the contextual meaning of words will naturally struggle with these cases, and the high number of these errors suggests that improving the semantic change detection may not have as large of an impact compared to including better contextual representations of potentially offensive words. The next most common category of misclassified offensive was self-deprecating statements: those that used statements that *would* be considered offensive had they been targeted at someone else, but they were instead directed at the author of the text (e.g., "I am ugly"). A few statements misclassified as offensive actually employed irony, in which the surface meaning of the text appears offensive, but the intended meaning of the text was not offensive.

For texts misclassified as not offensive, the most commonly noticed feature was that an offensive word was present, but it was not included in the offensive word list that was used by the best performing model. Some of these words acquired

Table 6: Analysis of error categories. The columns represent the category of error agreed upon by two annotators; the second and third column contain the incorrect prediction by our model and the last column contains the total counts.

Error category	NOT	OFF	Total
offensive-related words not used in an offensive way	0	96	96
offensive word not in list	20	0	20
self-deprecating	1	18	19
indirect offense	10	6	16
incorrect groundtruth	9	3	12
other/unexplained	5	7	12
irony	0	2	2

an offensive meaning over time. An example is "@USER I thought you magas refused to use Nike because they don't hate black people". In this tweet, the word *magas* is a case of a semantically-changed word which here is employed in an offensive way. In Urban Dictionary, this word is defined in November 2018 as "a word used in the campaign of trump, signals neo nazis and white supremacists". For these examples, we hypothesize that better expansion of the offensive word list may help with being able to correctly categorize these examples. For both types of misclassification, a handful of the instances contained more indirect examples of offense, which has been highlighted as an important category to focus on within the offense detection domain that may require multi-hop reasoning (Zhang et al., 2022). A small number of other examples appear to have been incorrectly labeled in the original dataset, and a handful were difficult to categorize (other) or understand (unexplained).

7 Conclusion

We have presented a study on combining lexical semantic change information into a new system that performs offensive language detection based on lexical features, and a curated gold standard list of English words that acquired or lost an offensive meaning between 2019 and 2020. From the point of view of the performance, our system trained on the much smaller and older OLID data performs better than SINAI trained on the same data. Further, by including our time-dependent lexical features, our system, trained only on the older OLID data, has performance on the newer SOLID test set that is comparable to a SINAI model that was trained directly on the much larger and newer SOLID training set. This shows that it indeed language change affects offensive language and it is possible to perform offensive language detection by taking into account such change and without relying on large labelled datasets that have been produced around the same time as the texts on which it is applied. Additionally, we discuss the challenges of performing short-term semantic change detection, especially for the rare words that acquired or lost an offensive meaning over a period of two years. Future work will involve expanding our evaluation across other time periods and corpora.

8 Acknowledgements

This work was supported by The Alan Turing Institute under the EPSRC grant EP/N510129/1. This research was supported in part through computational resources provided by The Alan Turing Institute and with the help of a generous gift from Microsoft Corporation. The work of Chiara Di Bonaventura was supported by UK Research and Innovation [grant number EP/S023356/1], in the UKRI Centre for Doctoral Training in Safe and Trusted Artificial Intelligence (www.safeandtrustedai.org). We would like to thank Dr Gard Jenset for his advice on the definition of the features and the study design and Madeline Tondi for curating the gold standard word list.

9 Author contributions

BMcG designed the study, managed and supervised the project. She also carried out the evaluation of the lexical semantic change module, the experiments with the offensive language detection module, refined the gold standard list and wrote Sections 1, 2.2, 3-3.3, 4.1, 5-5.2, and 6. JC reproduced the code for semantic change detection, contributed to the study design and wrote section 3.3. MA reproduced the code for offensive language detection and wrote Section 4. GT contributed to the design of the study and the supervision of the project; he wrote Section 2.1 and contributed to writing across the remaining sections. SW contributed to the design of the study and the supervision of the project, wrote part of Section 4.1, and helped edit the other sections. CDB contributed to Sections 2.1 and 6. AMP contributed to Sections 1 and 6. BMcG, MA, CDB, AMP, and SW performed the annotations used in section 6.

References

2021. "beta, n.". OED Online, Oxford University Press.

M Anand, Kishan Bhushan Sahay, Mohammed Altaf Ahmed, Daniyar Sultan, Radha Raman Chandan, and Bharat Singh. 2022. Deep learning and natural language processing in computation for offensive language detection in online social networks by feature selection and ensemble classification techniques. *Theoretical Computer Science*.

Pinar Arslan. 2020. Pin_cod_ at SemEval-2020 task 12: Injecting lexicons into bidirectional long short-term memory networks to detect Turkish offensive tweets. In *Proceedings of the Fourteenth Workshop on Semantic Evaluation*, pages 2117–2122, Barcelona (online). International Committee for Computational Linguistics.

Mikel Artetxe, Gorka Labaka, and Eneko Agirre. 2018. Generalizing and improving bilingual word embedding mappings with a multi-step framework of linear transformations. In *AAAI*.

Pinkesh Badjatiya, Shashank Gupta, Manish Gupta, and Vasudeva Varma. 2017. Deep Learning for Hate Speech Detection in Tweets. In *Proceedings of the 26th International Conference on World Wide Web Companion*, pages 759–760.

Pierpaolo Basile and Barbara McGillivray. 2018. *Discovery Science*, volume 11198 of *Lecture Notes in Computer Science*, chapter Exploiting the Web for Semantic Change Detection. Springer-Verlag.

Benjamin K. Bergen. 2016. The Science of Swear Words (Warning: NSFW AF). `https://www.wired.com/2016/09/science-swear-words-warning-nsfw-af/`. Accessed: 2021-08-26.

Steven Bird, Ewan Klein, and Edward Loper. 2009. *Natural language processing with Python: analyzing text with the natural language toolkit.* " O'Reilly Media, Inc.".

Tomas Brychcin, Stephen Eugene Taylor, and Lukas Svoboda. 2019. Cross-lingual word analogies using linear transformations between semantic spaces. *Expert Syst. Appl.*, 135:287–295.

Jacob Cohen. 1960. A coefficient of agreement for nominal scales. *Educational and Psychological Measurement*, (1):37–46.

Paul Cook, Jey Han Lau, Diana McCarthy, and Timothy Baldwin. 2014. Novel word-sense identification. In *Proceedings of COLING 2014, the 25th International Conference on Computational Linguistics: Technical Papers*, pages 1624–1635.

Thomas Davidson, Dana Warmsley, Michael Macy, and Ingmar Weber. 2017. Automated hate speech detection and the problem of offensive language. In *Eleventh International AAAI Conference on Web and Social Media*.

Jacob Devlin, Ming-Wei Chang, Kenton Lee, and Kristina Toutanova. 2019. BERT: Pre-training of deep bidirectional transformers for language understanding. In *Proceedings of the 2019 Conference of the North American Chapter of the Association for Computational Linguistics: Human Language Technologies, Volume 1 (Long and Short Papers)*, pages 4171–4186, Minneapolis, Minnesota. Association for Computational Linguistics.

Haim Dubossarsky, Simon Hengchen, Nina Tahmasebi, and Dominik Schlechtweg. 2019. Time-out: Temporal referencing for robust modeling of lexical semantic change. In *Proceedings of the 57th Annual Meeting of the Association for Computational Linguistics (Volume 1: Long Papers)*, Florence, Italy. Association for Computational Linguistics.

Haim Dubossarsky, Daphna Weinshall, and Eitan Grossman. 2017. Outta control: Laws of semantic change and inherent biases in word representation models. In *Proceedings of the 2017 Conference on Empirical Methods in Natural Language Processing*, pages 1136–1145.

Fatima-zahra El-Alami, Said Ouatik El Alaoui, and Noureddine En Nahnahi. 2022. A multilingual offensive language detection method based on transfer learning from transformer fine-tuning model. *Journal of King Saud University-Computer and Information Sciences*, 34(8):6048–6056.

Mai ElSherief, Vivek Kulkarni, Dana Nguyen, William Y. Wang, and Elizabeth Belding. 2018a. Hate lingo: A target-based linguistic analysis of hate speech in social media. In *Proceedings of the 12th International AAAI Conference on Web and Social Media*, ICWSM '18.

Mai ElSherief, Shirin Nilizadeh, Dana Nguyen, Giovanni Vigna, and Elizabeth Belding. 2018b. Peer to peer hate: Hate instigators and their targets. In *Proceedings of the 12th International AAAI Conference on Web and Social Media*, ICWSM '18.

Antigoni Maria Founta, Constantinos Djouvas, Despoina Chatzakou, Ilias Leontiadis, Jeremy Blackburn, Gianluca Stringhini, Athena Vakali, Michael Sirivianos, and Nicolas Kourtellis. 2018. Large scale crowdsourcing and characterization of twitter abusive behavior. In *Twelfth International AAAI Conference on Web and Social Media*.

Lea Frermann and Mirella Lapata. 2016. A Bayesian model of diachronic meaning change. *Transactions of the Association for Computational Linguistics*, 4:31–45.

Björn Gambäck and Utpal Kumar Sikdar. 2017. Using convolutional neural networks to classify hate-speech. In *Proceedings of the first workshop on abusive language online*, pages 85–90.

Joshua Garland, Keyan Ghazi-Zahedi, Jean-Gabriel Young, Laurent Hébert-Dufresne, and Mirta Galesic. 2020. Countering hate on social media: Large scale classification of hate and counter speech. In *Proceedings of the Fourth Workshop on Online Abuse and Harms*, pages 102–112.

Ella Guest, Bertie Vidgen, Alexandros Mittos, Nishanth Sastry, Gareth Tyson, and Helen Margetts. 2021. An expert annotated dataset for the detection of online misogyny. In *Proceedings of the 16th Conference of the European Chapter of the Association for Computational Linguistics: Main Volume*, pages 1336–1350.

Rishav Hada, Sohi Sudhir, Pushkar Mishra, Helen Yannakoudakis, Saif M Mohammad, and Ekaterina Shutova. 2021. Ruddit: Norms of offensiveness for english reddit comments. *arXiv preprint arXiv:2106.05664*.

William L Hamilton, Jure Leskovec, and Dan Jurafsky. 2016. Diachronic word embeddings reveal statistical laws of semantic change. In *Proceedings of the 54th Annual Meeting of the Association for Computational Linguistics*, volume 1, pages 1489–1501.

Manoel Horta Ribeiro, Pedro Calais, Yuri Santos, Virgílio Almeida, and Wagner Meira Jr. 2018. Characterizing and detecting hateful users on twitter. In *Proceedings of the International AAAI Conference on Web and Social Media*.

Adam Jatowt, Ricardo Campos, Sourav S Bhowmick, Nina Tahmasebi, and Antoine Doucet. 2018. Every word has its history: Interactive exploration and visualization of word sense evolution. In *Proceedings of the 27th ACM International Conference on Information and Knowledge Management*, pages 1899–1902. ACM.

Mladen Karan and Jan Šnajder. 2018. Cross-domain detection of abusive language online. In *Proceedings of the 2nd workshop on Abusive Language Online (ALW2)*, pages 132–137.

Yoon Kim, Yi-I Chiu, Kentaro Hanaki, Darshan Hegde, and Slav Petrov. 2014. Temporal analysis of language through neural language models. In *LTCSS at ACL*, pages 61–65.

M. Koptjevskaja-Tamm. 2002. The lexical typology of semantic shifts.

Vivek Kulkarni, Rami Al-Rfou, Bryan Perozzi, and Steven Skiena. 2015. Statistically significant detection of linguistic change. In *Proceedings of the 24th International Conference on World Wide Web*, pages 625–635. International World Wide Web Conferences Steering Committee.

Andrey Kutuzov, Erik Velldal, and Lilja Øvrelid. 2022. Contextualized embeddings for semantic change detection: Lessons learned. *Northern European Journal of Language Technology*, 8(1).

Zhenzhong Lan, Mingda Chen, Sebastian Goodman, Kevin Gimpel, Piyush Sharma, and Radu Soricut. 2019. Albert: A lite bert for self-supervised learning of language representations. In *International Conference on Learning Representations*.

Jey Han Lau, Paul Cook, Diana McCarthy, Spandana Gella, and Timothy Baldwin. 2014. Learning word sense distributions, detecting unattested senses and identifying novel senses using topic models. In *Proceedings of the 52nd Annual Meeting of the Association for Computational Linguistics (Volume 1: Long Papers)*, volume 1, pages 259–270.

Younghun Lee, Seunghyun Yoon, and Kyomin Jung. 2018. Comparative studies of detecting abusive language on twitter. *arXiv preprint arXiv:1808.10245*.

Yinhan Liu, Myle Ott, Naman Goyal, Jingfei Du, Mandar Joshi, Danqi Chen, Omer Levy, Mike Lewis, Luke Zettlemoyer, and Veselin Stoyanov. 2019. Roberta: A robustly optimized bert pretraining approach. *arXiv preprint arXiv:1907.11692*.

Sunny Mitra, Ritwik Mitra, Suman Kalyan Maity, Martin Riedl, Chris Biemann, Pawan Goyal, and Animesh Mukherjee. 2015. An automatic approach to identify word sense changes in text media across timescales. *Natural Language Engineering*, 21(5):773–798.

Alexandros Mittos, Savvas Zannettou, Jeremy Blackburn, and Emiliano De Cristofaro. 2020. "and we will fight for our race!" a measurement study of genetic testing conversations on reddit and 4chan. In *Proceedings of the International AAAI Conference on Web and Social Media*, volume 14, pages 452–463.

Marzieh Mozafari, Reza Farahbakhsh, and Noel Crespi. 2019. A bert-based transfer learning approach for hate speech detection in online social media. In *International Conference on Complex Networks and Their Applications*, pages 928–940.

Raphael Ottoni, Evandro Cunha, Gabriel Magno, Pedro Bernardina, Wagner Meira Jr, and Virgílio Almeida. 2018. Analyzing right-wing youtube channels: Hate, violence and discrimination. In *Proceedings of the 10th ACM conference on web science*, pages 323–332.

Flor Miriam Plaza-del Arco, M. Dolores Molina-González, Maite Martin, and L. Alfonso Ureña-López. 2019. SINAI at SemEval-2019 task 6: Incorporating lexicon knowledge into SVM learning to identify and categorize offensive language in social media. In *Proceedings of the 13th International Workshop on Semantic Evaluation*, pages 735–738, Minneapolis, Minnesota, USA. Association for Computational Linguistics.

Flor Miriam Plaza del Arco, M. Dolores Molina González, Alfonso Ureña-López, and Maite Martin. 2020. SINAI at SemEval-2020 task

12: Offensive language identification exploring transfer learning models. In *Proceedings of the Fourteenth Workshop on Semantic Evaluation*, pages 1622–1627, Barcelona (online). International Committee for Computational Linguistics.

Marco Polignano, Pierpaolo Basile, Marco De Gemmis, and Giovanni Semeraro. 2019. Hate speech detection through alberto italian language understanding model. In *NL4AI@ AI* IA*.

Ondřej Pražák, Pavel Přibáň, Stephen Taylor, and Jakub Sido. 2020. UWB at SemEval-2020 task 1: Lexical semantic change detection. In *Proceedings of the Fourteenth Workshop on Semantic Evaluation*, pages 246–254, Barcelona (online). International Committee for Computational Linguistics.

Alison Ribeiro and Nádia Silva. 2019. Inf-hateval at semeval-2019 task 5: Convolutional neural networks for hate speech detection against women and immigrants on twitter. In *Proceedings of the 13th International Workshop on Semantic Evaluation*, pages 420–425.

Alexander Robertson, Farhana Ferdousi Liza, Dong Nguyen, Barbara McGillivray, and Scott A. Hale. 2021. Semantic journeys: Quantifying change in emoji meaning from 2012–2018. In *Workshop Proceedings of the 15th International AAAI Conference on Web and Social Media*, online.

Sara Rosenthal, Pepa Atanasova, Georgi Karadzhov, Marcos Zampieri, and Preslav Nakov. 2020. A Large-Scale Semi-Supervised Dataset for Offensive Language Identification. page 14.

Maja Rudolph and David Blei. 2018. Dynamic embeddings for language evolution. In *Proceedings of the 2018 World Wide Web Conference on World Wide Web*, pages 1003–1011.

Dominik Schlechtweg, Barbara McGillivray, Simon Hengchen, Haim Dubossarsky, and Nina Tahmasebi. 2020. SemEval-2020 task 1: Unsupervised lexical semantic change detection. In *Proceedings of the Fourteenth Workshop on Semantic Evaluation*, pages 1–23, Barcelona (online). International Committee for Computational Linguistics.

Sumer Singh and Sheng Li. 2021. Exploiting auxiliary data for offensive language detection with bidirectional transformers. In *Proceedings of the 5th Workshop on Online Abuse and Harms (WOAH 2021)*, pages 1–5, Online. Association for Computational Linguistics.

Hajung Sohn and Hyunju Lee. 2019. Mc-bert4hate: Hate speech detection using multi-channel bert for different languages and translations. In *2019 International Conference on Data Mining Workshops (ICDMW)*, pages 551–559. IEEE.

Nina Tahmasebi. 2018. A study on word2vec on a historical Swedish newspaper corpus. In *CEUR Workshop Proceedings. Vol. 2084. Proceedings of the Digital Humanities in the Nordic Countries 3rd Conference, Helsinki Finland, March 7-9, 2018.*, Helsinki. University of Helsinki, Faculty of Arts.

Nina Tahmasebi, L. Borin, and A. Jatowt. 2018. Survey of computational approaches to lexical semantic change. *arXiv: Computation and Language*.

Nina Tahmasebi and Thomas Risse. 2017. Finding individual word sense changes and their delay in appearance. In *Proceedings of the International Conference Recent Advances in Natural Language Processing, RANLP 2017*, pages 741–749.

Xuri Tang. 2018. A state-of-the-art of semantic change computation. *Natural Language Engineering*, 24(5):649–676.

Zeerak Waseem, Thomas Davidson, Dana Warmsley, and Ingmar Weber. 2017. Understanding Abuse: A Typology of Abusive Language Detection Subtasks. *arXiv preprint arXiv:1705.09899*.

Zeerak Waseem and Dirk Hovy. 2016. Hateful Symbols or Hateful People? Predictive Features for Hate Speech Detection on Twitter. In *Proceedings of the NAACL Student Research Workshop*, pages 88–93.

Gregor Wiedemann, Seid Muhie Yimam, and Chris Biemann. 2020. UHH-LT at SemEval-2020 task 12: Fine-tuning of pre-trained transformer networks for offensive language detection. In *Proceedings of the Fourteenth Workshop on Semantic Evaluation*, pages 1638–1644, Barcelona (online). International Committee for Computational Linguistics.

Marcos Zampieri, Shervin Malmasi, Preslav Nakov, Sara Rosenthal, Noura Farra, and Ritesh Kumar. 2019a. Predicting the type and target of offensive posts in social media. pages 1415–1420.

Marcos Zampieri, Shervin Malmasi, Preslav Nakov, Sara Rosenthal, Noura Farra, and Ritesh Kumar. 2019b. Semeval-2019 task 6: Identifying and categorizing offensive language in social media (offenseval). In *Proceedings of the 13th International Workshop on Semantic Evaluation*, pages 75–86.

Marcos Zampieri, Preslav Nakov, Sara Rosenthal, Pepa Atanasova, Georgi Karadzhov, Hamdy Mubarak, Leon Derczynski, Zeses Pitenis, and Çağrı Çöltekin. 2020. SemEval-2020 task 12: Multilingual offensive language identification in social media (OffensEval 2020). In *Proceedings of the Fourteenth Workshop on Semantic Evaluation*, pages 1425–1447, Barcelona (online). International Committee for Computational Linguistics.

Qiang Zhang, Jason Naradowsky, and Yusuke Miyao. 2022. Rethinking offensive text detection as a multi-hop reasoning problem. In *Findings of the Association for Computational Linguistics: ACL 2022*, pages 3888–3905, Dublin, Ireland. Association for Computational Linguistics.

Ziqi Zhang, David Robinson, and Jonathan Tepper. 2018. Detecting hate speech on twitter using a convolution-gru based deep neural network. In *European semantic web conference*, pages 745–760. Springer.

A Appendix

Table 7: Gold standard list of words that acquired an offensive sense for which there is evidence in our 2020 corpus (left) and stable words (right). For each group, the first column provides the part of speech, the second the lemma, the third the frequency in the 2019 Twitter corpus and the fourth the frequency in the 2020 Twitter corpus.

pos	Lemma	Freq 2019	Freq 2020	Stable word	Freq 2019	Freq 2020
N	beta	49	67	academy	50	65
ADJ	cancel	25	64	acceptable	23	63
N	cap	153	221	fish	151	228
ADJ	cringe	36	65	additional	33	72
N	fag	15	20	accuracy	16	17
N	globalist	17	21	absurd	23	23
N	karen	39	106	behaviour	48	99
N	monkey	60	97	corporation	59	99
N	mug	68	93	cage	62	85
N	ratchet	2	12	moonstone	2	3
ADJ	salty	17	31	alcoholic	19	22
N	simp	5	67	whorehouse	5	63
N	skip	155	148	abandonment	5	10
N	snowflake	11	27	calamity	2	19
ADJ	sus	11	24	beneficial	8	20
ADJ	thirsty	33	35	dreamy	26	29
N	illegal	170	217	direction	163	223
N	chad	8	23	contestant	9	213
N	gammon	4	6	gravel	3	8
N	Brexiter	1	9	grenade	3	12
ADJ	triggered	31	31	analytic	27	39

Table 8: Gold standard list of words that acquired an offensive meaning, the date of its first recorded usage and the source dictionary.

pos	Lemma	Offensive meaning	Source	Date
N	beta	Insult describing a man who is seen as passive, subservient, weak, and effeminate.	https://www.dictionary.com/e/slang/beta/	1990
ADJ	canceled	When a person is canceled, they are no longer supported publicly. Sometimes used as a threat, "to cancel."	https://www.dictionary.com/e/pop-culture/cancel-culture/	2015
N	cap	A lie.	https://www.urbandictionary.com/define.php?term=cap	2020
ADJ	cringe	Someone or something extremely embarrassing or awkward.	https://www.urbandictionary.com/define.php?term=Cringe	2013
N	fag	A derogatory term for homosexual.	https://www.urbandictionary.com/define.php?term=fag	2010
N	globalist	Coded language often used as a negative euphemism for Jew.	https://www.urbandictionary.com/define.php?term=Globalist	2018
N	karen	Karen is a pejorative slang term for an obnoxious, angry, entitled, and often racist middle-aged white woman who uses her privilege to get her way or police other people's behaviors.	https://www.dictionary.com/e/slang/karen/	2020
N	monkey	A derogatory term for a black person.	https://www.urbandictionary.com/define.php?term=Monkey	2011
N	mug	Unattractive, unappealing, or unpleasant.	https://oed.com/view/Entry/89666161?rskey=Vq0ZKB&result=0&isAdvanced=true#firstMatch	2009
N	ratchet	Someone whose actions could be considered as severely undistinguishable; possesing little or no class.	https://oed.com/view/Entry/89666161?rskey=Vq0ZKB&result=0&isAdvanced=true#firstMatch	2009
ADJ	salty	Angry, upset, or hostile, especially due to embarrassment or failure.	https://www.dictionary.com/browse/salty	2011
N	simp	Simp is a slang insult for men who are seen as too attentive and submissive to women, especially out of a failed hope of winning some entitled sexual attention or activity from them. Can also refer to an avid fan of a celebrity.	https://www.dictionary.com/e/slang/simp/	2011
N	skip	A white Australian, alluding to Skippy the Bush Kangaroo, a once-popular Australian television show for children.	https://www.dictionary.com/browse/salty	2011
N	snowflake	A political insult for someone who is perceived as too sensitive, often used against young people and those with progressive political viewpoints.	https://www.dictionary.com/browse/snowflake	2015
ADJ	sus	Giving the impression that something is questionable or dishonest; suspicious.	https://www.dictionary.com/browse/snowflake	2015
ADJ	thirsty	Describes a graceless need for approval, affection or attention, to the point of another becoming uncomfortable.	https://www.dictionary.com/browse/snowflake	2015
N	illegal	Derogatory term for a Hispanic or Latino person in the United States.	https://www.dictionary.com/browse/snowflake	2015
N	chad	A rude, and often sexually promiscuous, man.	https://www.urbandictionary.com/define.php?term=Chad&page=4	2017
N	gammon	A term used against anyone who was white and voted for Brexit.	https://www.urbandictionary.com/define.php?term=Gammon	2018
N	Brexiter	An derogatory term to refer to someone who voted for Brexit.	https://www.urbandictionary.com/define.php?term=Brexiter	2016
ADJ	triggered	An emotional/psychological reaction caused by something that somehow relates to an upsetting time or happening in someone's life.	https://www.urbandictionary.com/define.php?term=Triggered	2016

Table 9: Pairwise Inter-Annotator Agreement (IAA) scores for the error analysis.

Annotators	**IAA**
A_1 & A_2	0.53 (moderate)
A_2 & A_3	0.88 (strong)
A_1 & A_3	0.09 (disagreement)
A_2 & A_4	0.39 (fair)
A_4 & A_5	0.40 (fair)
A_3 & A_5	0.37 (fair)
A_3 & A_4	0.56 (moderate)
A_1 & A_4	0.46 (moderate)

Temporal Word Meaning Disambiguation using TimeLMs

Mihir Godbole* and **Parth Dandavate*** and **Aditya Kane***
Pune Institute of Computer Technology, Pune
{mihirgod11, dandavateparth, adityakane1}@gmail.com

Abstract

Meaning of words constantly change given the events in modern civilization. Large Language Models use word embeddings, which are often static and thus cannot cope with this semantic change. Thus,it is important to resolve ambiguity in word meanings. This paper is an effort in this direction, where we explore methods for word sense disambiguation for the EvoNLP shared task. We conduct rigorous ablations for two solutions to this problem. We see that an approach using time-aware language models helps this task. Furthermore, we explore possible future directions to this problem.

1 Introduction

A change in the meaning of a word in varying semantic contents is a challenge for various NLP tasks such as text and sentence classification, question answering and sentence prediction. Recent developments in large language models (LLMs) like ELMo (Peters et al., 2018), BERT (Devlin et al., 2019) and GPT (Brown et al., 2020) have revolutionised the field of NLP with context dependent word embeddings. These models have been trained on a large corpus of unlabelled text. While these models take in consideration the semantics of the text, it is limited to the corpus it was trained on. This introduces a new challenge of the shift in the meaning of a word across the temporal axis.

Word Sense Disambiguation (Huang et al., 2019) is the process of identifying the meaning of a word from multiple possible meanings in varying contexts. This task can be further extended as a polysemy resolution task to classify the meaning of words in different contexts. Our system performs a similar task while classifying two texts with a common word with the same or different meaning. Specifically, the premise of our system is to classify tweets from two different time periods with a common word. The variation in the meaning of a word is caused by two factors, the context of the word in the form of a tweet or a change in the usage and hence in the meaning of a word because of the shift along the time axis. Historically it has been observed that the meanings of some words have been altered over time. For example, the word "fathom" originally meant "to encircle with one's arms" and now is defined as "to understand after much thought". The ever expanding nature of the internet and social media have led to rapid evolution of words, with the meanings of words changing and new words getting csoined. This means that the corpus of data used for training a LLM will keep changing over time. Hence, the pretrained models for existing LLMs like BERT, RoBERTa cannot be used to compare word embeddings for a word from two different time periods. This shared task (Loureiro et al., 2022b) focusses precisely on this problem statement.

To address this problem, we propose a system comprising of TimeLMs (Loureiro et al., 2022a) to incorporate the time aspect of the data. TimeLMs are language models that are trained using data up to a certain time instance. In this case they are trained on tweets gathered by the end of a year. Therefore there exists a unique TimeLM model for each year which takes into account the time aspect of data. The dataset used for testing our system consists of tweets from the years 2019, 2020 and 2021. Tweets from two different time periods containing a common word are paired in this dataset and labelled to indicate similarity or dissimilarity in the meanings of that word in the two tweets. The TimeLMs used in our system are Roberta models trained on tweets upto the specific year. This enables our system to get an accurate representations of the words based on their use upto that time period. The embeddings are then compared based on a similarity metric to classify the tweets using a preset threshold value for similarity.

*Equal Contribution

Proceedings of the The First Workshop on Ever Evolving NLP (EvoNLP), pages 55 - 60
December 7, 2022 ©2022 Association for Computational Linguistics

This paper is organised as follows. We analyse existing research and methods in Section (2). We give a overview of the dataset used for our system in Section (3). We provide a overview of our system implementation in Section (4). We also compare the results of our experiments in developing this system in Section (5). We discuss the possible improvements and scope of this system in Section (6).

2 Related work

In Natural Language Processing, the meaning of words is denoted by a vector, commonly known as word embedding. Works like GloVe (Pennington et al., 2014) and Word2Vec (Mikolov et al., 2013) were one of the first ones to represent a word using vectors. However, the embeddings thus generated were context-agnostic, meaning their meaning was fixed and were not dependent on the context.

With the dawn of modern text encoders (Vaswani et al., 2017; Devlin et al., 2019), context dependent embeddings can be easily calculated. Works like Pilehvar and Camacho-Collados; Raganato et al. aim to have manually annotated datasets containing pairs of sentences having same or different meaning, and labelling them as such. To solve this task, several methods have been developed. Works like Levine et al. (2020); Peters et al. (2019) try to impart context based knowledge into the embeddings by using WordNet (Miller, 1995) attributes. The models are trained in a self-supervised fashion with entity linking. Another approach is to use word-level embeddings. Loureiro and Jorge (2019) use this approach, combining it with a k-NN (k Nearest Neighbours) method to disambiguate the word embeddings. Note that transformers can also be used for this purpose, since the output features from the transformers can be interpreted as word embeddings. Loureiro et al. (2022c) studies model layers to understand the effect of attention-based architectures in word sense disambiguation task. Elmo (Peters et al., 2018) is one of many available architectures in this direction. Lastly, work has been done to incorporate the semantic space knowledge into the embeddings (Colla et al., 2020), also known as sense-based disambiguation.

Given this, little work has been done on word meaning disambiguation in a temporal setting. This means that the information about the time of text utterance is also provided along with the sentence itself. This paper tries to provide a solution to this problem - word meaning disambiguation when temporal information is available.

3 Dataset description

The dataset consists of 1428 training samples and 396 validation samples. The final scores were calculated on a set of 10,000 unseen test samples. In every training sample, we were provided with two sentences and the word whose semantic meaning was to be compared. Some metadata like tokens and start and end of word was also included in every sample.In the training dataset, out of the 1428 samples, 650 examples had the words in two sentences having same meaning, whereas 778 samples had the words in two sentences having different meaning. Note that since this dataset is relatively balanced, and hence does not need any additional preprocessing to balance the data distribution. However, it is important to note that the target words in the training and testing dataset constitute two different sets, and hence the problem should be solved in a way that is target word agnostic.

An illustration of the data is shown in Figure 1. The left part shows an example where the meaning of the target word "virus" is different in both tweets. Specifically, in the top left tweet it indicates to the disease-causing organism whereas the bottom left tweet indicates to a thing that the person likes. In the right part, both instances of the target word mean the same, denoting disease-causing organism.

The dataset also provides the month and year when the tweet was written. This provides us the temporal information, which can be useful for the semantic evaluation of the words in the given context. Our approach aims at using this semantic information in a way that a language model relevant to the tweet is used to get the semantic features of the tweet.

4 Methodology

4.1 TimeLMs aided word sense disambiguation

As mentioned in Section 3, the date of posting of the tweet is provided as a data attribute. In this approach, we used this information to choose the transformer model to extract target features. We use TimeLMs (Loureiro et al., 2022a) for this purpose. We observe this performs better compared to using a single model. Our method is illustrated in Figure 2.

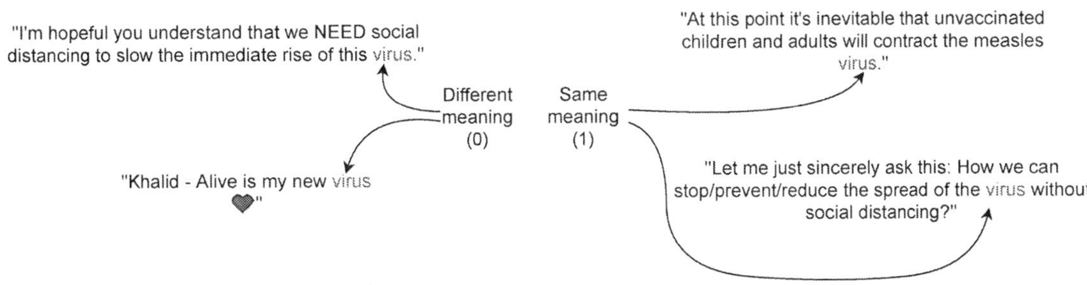

Figure 1: Examples from the datset.

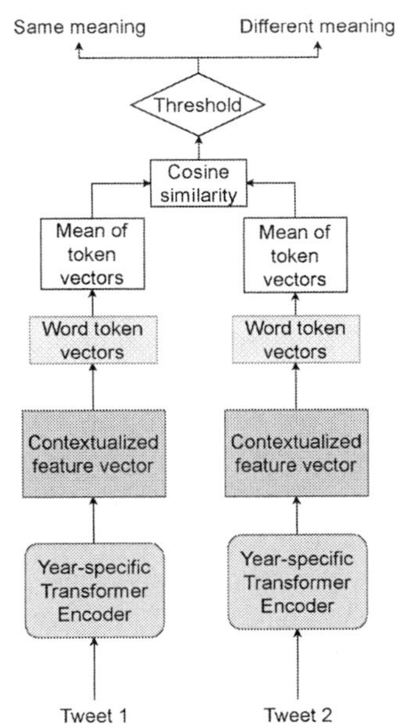

Figure 2: TimeLMs aided word sense disambiguation

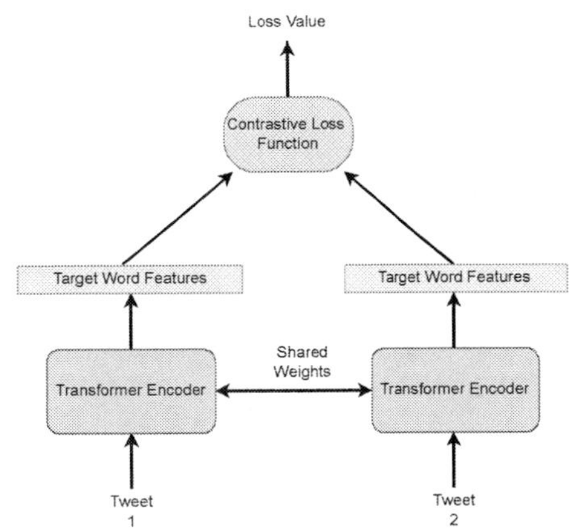

Figure 3: Contrastive feature based classification

Specifically, we observe that the tweets in the input data are posted in the years 2019 and 2020 only. Thus, we use the variants of TimeLMs trained on Twitter data collected until December 2019 and 2020 for respectively dated tweets. In this way, we can encapsulate the difference in semantic representations of sentences across time.

After extracting the contextualized sentence features from the respective models, we extract the target word features. We hereby get two word feature vectors, one corresponding to each tweet. Note that since one word may be split into multiple tokens, we use the mean of these token-wise features for out computation. Note that the feature vectors for a tweet is the mean of the last four layers of the language models concatenated to the pooled ($[CLS]$ token) output. These two feature vectors are then compared with each other using cosine similarity. If this cosine similarity is high, the meaning of the target word in two sentences is the same, alternatively if the cosine similarity is low then the meaning of the target word in the two sentences is different.

Since this approach does not actually train the parameters of the model, we use the training dataset to calculate the thresholds. Specifically, we iterate over potential thresholds between 0 and 1 with a step of 0.001. We then rank the thresholds based on their F1 scores. The best performing threshold is then used for generating the final predictions. The threshold for our best performing model (TimeLMs) was 0.917. We use five models for our ablations: ELECTRA (small) (Clark et al., 2020), ALBERT (base) (Lan et al., 2019), BERT (base, uncased) (Devlin et al., 2019), RoBERTa (base) (Zhuang et al., 2021), TimeLMs (Loureiro et al., 2022a).

4.2 Contrastive feature based classification

The task essentially being identifying whether the usage of word is similar or not we thought of training the language models in a Siamese setting. Siamese networks involves two similar encoder networks with the same weights and a classification system, which determines the similarity based on the distance between encoded features and a threshold. As mentioned in the previous sub section we are extracting the target word features using transformer models which will be the encoders. If the meaning of the word in both the sentences is same then the target word features given by the transformer model should be similar.

We trained the model using a simple contrastive loss involving euclidean distance between the target word features. We used the same models as mentions in the previous sections, except for the TimeLMs. For determining the threshold for the classification process we iterated through a range of 0 to 4, with a step of 0.01, while testing on the validation data. The threshold was determined for the euclidean distance between the word embeddings obtained from the model. The threshold for our best performing model (TimeLMs) was 1.148.

4.3 Implementation details

We use the HuggingFace library (Wolf et al., 2020) for our experiments. For the cosine similarity experiments, we find a threshold of 0.917 for our best performing solution. We use a batch size of 64. Here the threshold was selected for the cosine distance between the two word embeddings.

For the contrastive method experiments, we find a threshold of 1.148 for our best performing solution (RoBERTa). We used a batch size of 8. Here the threshold was selected for the euclidean distance between the two word embeddings.

In both cases, the inference distance value (cosine or euclidean) below the threshold indicated similar meaning for the two words, and the the inference distance value above the threshold indicated different meaning for the two words.

5 Results

We hereby present the results of both of our methods. We report several interesting observations based on the results.

Our results based on our cosine similarity are shown in Table 1 and our results based on the contrastive method are shown in Table 2.

Model	Val F1-score	Val Accuracy	Test F1-score
Electra	61.00	54.78	38.77
RoBERTa	60.00	56.51	38.96
BERT	60.80	56.77	38.77
Albert	60.73	56.77	39.00
TimeLMs	**61**	**61.71**	**57.94**

Table 1: Results of Similarity Method

Model	Val F1-score	Val Accuracy	Test F1-score
Electra	**66.67**	**75**	46.15
RoBERTa	60.8	44.01	**48.97**
BERT	65.44	48.98	44.34
Albert	66.6	66.6	43.75

Table 2: Results of Contrastive Method

1. **TimeLMs based method performs the best:** We observe that the TimeLMs based method performs the best. We speculate this is because of the time-aware nature of the models. Some words, for example "lockdown" have significantly different meaning before and after the pandemix. Thus, models pretrained on the specific data results in better performance.

2. **BERT and AlBERT have similar performance:** We see that BERT and Albert have very similar Accuracy and Macro-F1. We hypothesize that this is because of the similarity in their pretraining objectives. Albert is a model aimed to mimic the capabilities of BERT, but with lower number of parameters. Thus, it makes sense that these models have very similar validation metrics.

3. **Electra has a better language representation:** As seen on state of art benchmarks like GLUE and SQuAD Electra is outperforming RoBERTa, ALBERT. Electra has achieved better F1-score and accuracy compared to both.

6 Conclusion

In this paper, we explore two solutions to the word sense disambiguation problem within the scope of EvoNLP shared task. We report a maximum testing F1-score of 57.94% with TimeLMs. We foresee several research directions for this work. One line of work can be explore robustness of the contrastive models. The threshold search technique for this method can be explored in greater detail.

References

Tom B Brown, Benjamin Mann, Nick Ryder, Melanie Subbiah, Jared Kaplan, Prafulla Dhariwal, Arvind Neelakantan, Pranav Shyam, Girish Sastry, Amanda Askell, et al. 2020. Language models are few-shot learners. *arXiv preprint arXiv:2005.14165*.

Kevin Clark, Minh-Thang Luong, Quoc V. Le, and Christopher D. Manning. 2020. ELECTRA: pre-training text encoders as discriminators rather than generators. In *8th International Conference on Learning Representations, ICLR 2020, Addis Ababa, Ethiopia, April 26-30, 2020*. OpenReview.net.

Davide Colla, Enrico Mensa, and Daniele P. Radicioni. 2020. LessLex: Linking multilingual embeddings to SenSe representations of LEXical items. *Computational Linguistics*, 46(2):289–333.

Jacob Devlin, Ming-Wei Chang, Kenton Lee, and Kristina Toutanova. 2019. BERT: Pre-training of deep bidirectional transformers for language understanding. In *Proceedings of the 2019 Conference of the North American Chapter of the Association for Computational Linguistics: Human Language Technologies, Volume 1 (Long and Short Papers)*, pages 4171–4186, Minneapolis, Minnesota. Association for Computational Linguistics.

Luyao Huang, Chi Sun, Xipeng Qiu, and Xuanjing Huang. 2019. GlossBERT: BERT for word sense disambiguation with gloss knowledge. In *Proceedings of the 2019 Conference on Empirical Methods in Natural Language Processing and the 9th International Joint Conference on Natural Language Processing (EMNLP-IJCNLP)*, pages 3509–3514, Hong Kong, China. Association for Computational Linguistics.

Zhenzhong Lan, Mingda Chen, Sebastian Goodman, Kevin Gimpel, Piyush Sharma, and Radu Soricut. 2019. Albert: A lite bert for self-supervised learning of language representations.

Yoav Levine, Barak Lenz, Or Dagan, Ori Ram, Dan Padnos, Or Sharir, Shai Shalev-Shwartz, Amnon Shashua, and Yoav Shoham. 2020. SenseBERT: Driving some sense into BERT. In *Proceedings of the 58th Annual Meeting of the Association for Computational Linguistics*, pages 4656–4667, Online. Association for Computational Linguistics.

Daniel Loureiro, Francesco Barbieri, Leonardo Neves, Luis Espinosa Anke, and Jose Camacho-collados. 2022a. TimeLMs: Diachronic language models from Twitter. In *Proceedings of the 60th Annual Meeting of the Association for Computational Linguistics: System Demonstrations*, pages 251–260, Dublin, Ireland. Association for Computational Linguistics.

Daniel Loureiro, Aminette D'Souza, Areej Nasser Muhajab, Isabella A. White, Gabriel Wong, Luis Espinosa-Anke, Leonardo Neves, Francesco Barbieri, and Jose Camacho-Collados. 2022b. TempoWiC: An evaluation benchmark for detecting meaning shift in social media. In *Proceedings of the 29th International Conference on Computational Linguistics*, pages 3353–3359, Gyeongju, Republic of Korea. International Committee on Computational Linguistics.

Daniel Loureiro and Alípio Jorge. 2019. Language modelling makes sense: Propagating representations through WordNet for full-coverage word sense disambiguation. In *Proceedings of the 57th Annual Meeting of the Association for Computational Linguistics*, pages 5682–5691, Florence, Italy. Association for Computational Linguistics.

Daniel Loureiro, Al'ipio M'ario Jorge, and José Camacho-Collados. 2022c. Lmms reloaded: Transformer-based sense embeddings for disambiguation and beyond. *Artif. Intell.*, 305:103661.

Tomas Mikolov, Kai Chen, Greg Corrado, and Jeffrey Dean. 2013. Efficient estimation of word representations in vector space.

George A. Miller. 1995. Wordnet: A lexical database for english. *Commun. ACM*, 38(11):39–41.

Jeffrey Pennington, Richard Socher, and Christopher D. Manning. 2014. Glove: Global vectors for word representation. In *Empirical Methods in Natural Language Processing (EMNLP)*, pages 1532–1543.

Matthew E. Peters, Mark Neumann, Mohit Iyyer, Matt Gardner, Christopher Clark, Kenton Lee, and Luke Zettlemoyer. 2018. Deep contextualized word representations. In *Proceedings of the 2018 Conference of the North American Chapter of the Association for Computational Linguistics: Human Language Technologies, Volume 1 (Long Papers)*, pages 2227–2237, New Orleans, Louisiana. Association for Computational Linguistics.

Matthew E. Peters, Mark Neumann, Robert Logan, Roy Schwartz, Vidur Joshi, Sameer Singh, and Noah A. Smith. 2019. Knowledge enhanced contextual word representations. In *Proceedings of the 2019 Conference on Empirical Methods in Natural Language Processing and the 9th International Joint Conference on Natural Language Processing (EMNLP-IJCNLP)*, pages 43–54, Hong Kong, China. Association for Computational Linguistics.

Mohammad Taher Pilehvar and José Camacho-Collados. 2018. Wic: 10, 000 example pairs for evaluating context-sensitive representations. *CoRR*, abs/1808.09121.

Alessandro Raganato, Tommaso Pasini, José Camacho-Collados, and Mohammad Taher Pilehvar. 2020. Xl-wic: A multilingual benchmark for evaluating semantic contextualization. *CoRR*, abs/2010.06478.

Ashish Vaswani, Noam Shazeer, Niki Parmar, Jakob Uszkoreit, Llion Jones, Aidan N Gomez, Ł ukasz Kaiser, and Illia Polosukhin. 2017. Attention is all you need. In *Advances in Neural Information Processing Systems*, volume 30. Curran Associates, Inc.

Thomas Wolf, Lysandre Debut, Victor Sanh, Julien Chaumond, Clement Delangue, Anthony Moi, Pierric Cistac, Tim Rault, Remi Louf, Morgan Funtowicz, Joe Davison, Sam Shleifer, Patrick von Platen, Clara Ma, Yacine Jernite, Julien Plu, Canwen Xu, Teven Le Scao, Sylvain Gugger, Mariama Drame, Quentin Lhoest, and Alexander Rush. 2020. Transformers: State-of-the-art natural language processing. In *Proceedings of the 2020 Conference on Empirical Methods in Natural Language Processing: System Demonstrations*, pages 38–45, Online. Association for Computational Linguistics.

Liu Zhuang, Lin Wayne, Shi Ya, and Zhao Jun. 2021. A robustly optimized BERT pre-training approach with post-training. In *Proceedings of the 20th Chinese National Conference on Computational Linguistics*, pages 1218–1227, Huhhot, China. Chinese Information Processing Society of China.

Author Index

Association for Computational Linguistics
209 N. Eighth Street
Stroudsburg, Pennsylvania 18360

ISBN 978-1-7138-9108-6

CURRAN ASSOCIATES INC.
proceedings
.com